STEPPING STONES
FOR SPIRITUAL SUCCESS

STEPPING STONES
FOR SPIRITUAL SUCCESS

By Taoist Master
Ni, Hua-Ching

The Shrine of the Eternal Breath of Tao
College of Tao and Traditional Chinese Healing
LOS ANGELES

Acknowledgement: Our thanks and appreciation to Liza Hughes, George Robinson and Janet DeCourtney for their help in editing and proofreading this book.

The Shrine of the Eternal Breath of Tao, Malibu, California
College of Tao and Traditional Chinese Healing,
117 Stonehaven Way
Los Angeles, CA 90049

Dedicated to
those who are developing
their most respectable and durable
personality in worldly life.

To female readers,

According to Taoist teaching, male and female are equally important in the natural sphere. This is seen in the diagram of Tai Chi. Thus, discrimination is not practiced in our tradition. All my work is dedicated to both genders of human people.

Wherever possible, situations of using masculine pronouns to present both sexes are avoided. Where they exist, we ask your tolerance and spiritual understanding. We hope that you will take the essence of my teaching and overlook the triviality of language. Gender discrimination is inherent in English; ancient Chinese pronouns do not have the difference of gender. I wish all of you might achieve yourselves above the level of language or gender.

Thank you, H.C. Ni

CONTENTS

PREFACE

SEVERAL MILLION years ago, human life appeared on earth. Around 2,000 to 3,000 years ago, in some societies, teachings were developed and organized externally called religions which hold the expectation of directing people's behavior and thoughts. The first of those establishments did not appear until about 3,000 years ago; they then attained dominance in society. They made no mention of spiritual faith. Before that cultural development, however, what was the nature of human societies? In their natural environments, did our ancestors attain any spiritual development, and what was their achievement? Human life in each succeeding generation needs to grow in its own way. No single generation which has attained maturity can force future generations to follow the same standard. So therefore, there is no way we can depend upon one generation to do the growing. No single generation can do the job for all the generations.

Here is an interesting story to illustrate the experience of growth of different societies. We can alternate between the eastern and western hemispheres of the globe to help us understand more. In northeastern Asia, the largest population is in China. In that country, one of the most favored wives of an emperor started the custom of binding her feet. By doing this, she was able to walk gracefully and was highly praised by the emperor. Afterwards, many women imitated her and bound their feet so they too could walk gracefully. For close to a thousand years, most women in China bound their feet. In the spring, some locales even held contests for the smallest feet. These historical facts do not convey, however, the pain and the tears suffered by the women. Yet women were obviously willing to endure the pain in order to look beautiful according to a set fashion.

In the West, people did not bind their feet, but they did bind their minds for some 1,500 to 1,700 years. In their spiritual development, the mind of Western society has been as restricted as the bound feet of the Chinese women. Western society has only recently been released from the mental bondage of culture and society and has not yet found or rediscovered the naturalness of the original mind.

It was a great liberation for the Chinese women to give up the custom of binding their feet and to return to having healthy, natural feet. It could also be a liberation for people in Western society to start slowly to untie their minds and restore the natural healthy mind. Being unnatural expresses a state of confusion where people do not know what is right. They do not accept themselves. Once they do, they become natural again, and their minds become clear. This progress is important. The evolution of the human spirit and thought is of much greater concern than any physical fashion of the day.

When it comes to the present, a young heart can be very busy in pursuing all kinds of wonders, many different achievements in the world, both eastern and western. In the West, the great achievements are machinery, communications and weapons. In the East, the great achievements are the high spiritual traditions, the high mystery of spiritual reality and the subtle performance of spiritual powers. It is all fascinating; it is all a great attraction to a young heart, but by pursuing them, it is easy to miss some of the basic foundations of life.

You know, many generations ago in the tradition of Tao, the ancestors attained Tao which is also called the integral truth or the path of internal and external growth through spiritual integration. Unfortunately, as each generation developed, they could not always nurture a balanced spiritual integration. Because they were attracted by external wonders, they extended themselves externally rather than maintaining their internal growth. The wonders pulled them outside of themselves, so they lost some of the fundamental inner realities that had been achieved by their ancestors. However, if a good foundation is built in young hearts, their development can be corrected.

There are some important guidelines to be learned and remembered through practicing recitation. It is useful and valuable to recite the fundamental achievements of our ancestors when you are both young and old. Those achievements will not limit your development; they provide you with a foundation so you can grow further. Spiritual learning is similar to technical achievement. Do you think the technically backward Eastern or African societies should begin making airplanes or computers on a trial and error basis, or should they go to the West to learn the technology that has already been developed? They could start from the Western foundation to look for further development, or start at the beginning, all over again.

Fortunately or unfortunately, we have seen that not all positive developments can be preserved. Sometimes they are lost, and sometimes a new idea will spring from it, bringing an even higher development. If a development is lost, then people have to start all over again. The use of the human mind is an exercise, but if we are fortunate enough to have a foundation upon which to build, it is beneficial and correct to make the effort to establish that foundation. That is better then starting over again.

Shamanism is one of mankind's earliest spiritual practices; it developed naturally in Asia and is still utilized by some tribes today. The shamanistic traditions in different regions have different features which basically represent a primitive stage of the spirit of the tribes. This is quite different from the spiritual understanding of the early ancestors of the Chinese people, who recognized the three divisions of natural authority: Heaven, earth and mankind. The ancient Chinese developed an art of managing the spirits that could harm human life. In other words, the art of Taoism concerns the governing of the internal and external spirits, while religions worship these spirits. Taoism developed from the ancient natural society. Its practices originated from the pursuit of immortality; all its discoveries, spiritual and material, were inspired by this single motivation in pursuit of immortality. It is a growth process that attains wisdom by means of natural spiritual development and intense spiritual practice. It encompasses many kinds of experiences and achievements, but they can be divided into two main segments. One aspect of Taoism is directed to highly achieved spiritual development and the other part is the practice of highly developed spiritual powers. Utilizing both, the mind of the practitioner develops based on a realistic foundation of spiritual experience and practice. This can only be gathered by refined spiritual practice. Can all descendants maintain such development? Not at all. The focus for most people is on competition or contention in the external pursuit of social or material glory.

Taoism is not totally lost, but its subtlety is understood, enjoyed and developed by only a limited number of aware people. The majority of people do not truly develop themselves, here or elsewhere. Taoism, and other high achievements of human society, was already lost long ago. Around 2,500 years ago in the area around China, spiritual teachers had to face a difficult time. They looked to the spiritual achievements of the past in an effort to help the new, confused society. Though they renewed the ancient teachings, those teachings were not totally understood, so they became the spiritual possession of only a few people.

It should be remembered that spiritual development cannot be achieved by utilizing unnatural approaches, like binding the feet of women. It should also be remembered that good spiritual achievement can not rely totally on the interpretation or operation of the intellectual or undeveloped mind. If such sources are used to program an individual or a society, the development of any individual or the majority of the people will be limited. Once people become followers of a rigid framework or conceptual perspective, spiritual development begins to wither. People who look for social positions and power will find that their spiritual development will be stunted. If there is no supporting scientific attitude to assist spiritual development, blind faith will be the result. First, objective spiritual facts need to be gathered through basic spiritual practice; later, it can develop into an art.

The forefathers of the teaching of Tao developed themselves in relation to a natural spiritual reality. A new generation that does not have as solid a foundation for growth as their fathers did cannot distinguish between true and false teachings. Following the establishment of social religion, people were put into a new state of bondage. When people are kept struggling in the fetters of religion rather than living in spiritual freedom, no truthful spiritual achievement will be attained.   Spiritual archetypes and roles have been respected and assimilated by people for centuries. People like to appear as noble and above others; they wanted to be rulers, great or petty, to personally share in the sovereignty of the archetypical religious framework. A leaders' ego desire for sovereignty and omnipotence is the true dynamic that pushed society into becoming unnatural.   Religion became the tool for leaders to accomplish that goal, and thus all societies have become unnatural.

During a time of confusion lasting many years, the Taoists, the followers of the unchanging simple spiritual essence, received a new cultural challenge and inspiration. In that time, they returned to the study of spiritual reality, to know how they began and where they were.   They developed a renewed Taoism; the distilled essence from millions of years of life experience and spiritual practice. So the teaching emerging in this book is evolving through the same process and is a further distillation from all ancient spiritual achievement.

Anyone who wishes to achieve themselves spiritually should work first on the foundation. So now we all may restore our original nature; we do not have to bind our minds any more. We can start from the right place, the achievement of the ancient developed ones. The natural way is to give you a foundation for your growth that offers you unlimited freedom to pursue and attain what you can be and what you can do. The royal jelly we present here is great nutrition; it is not a limitation.   I introduce it to you as what I have learned   from   our   naturally   developed   human ancestors.

I am glad the ancient developed ones provided us with good examples for us to follow and use in our everyday life. By following the way, as instructed by those achieved ones, all will be right, all is correct and all is fortunate. Without such guidance, our own trip of trial and error would be a waste of time, energy and resources. However, even with the guidance of the ancients, we still try, we still adventure, take risks and go forward in our lives of changes, but now, after studying the book, our trip is not purposeless or blind. We perceive the rationale for living a good, positive life. We have the proper instruction to live an effective life. The reason why we work on this is to serve ourselves. My beloved friends and readers, there is no need to waste your time, as have many people who have tried but failed. If we are wise, we will come back to the important fundamentals. With that learning, we can gather and enjoy the highest spiritual development from our own efforts. That is possible now.

I would like this book to serve as a mirror you might like to use in your life as your inner voice which will call you at those most important moments. This book is not produced by Heaven. It comes from the innermost room of your highest spiritual essence which connects you with the subtle light of Heaven.

Ni, Hua Ching
October 5, 1989

CHAPTER ONE

Live in the Light

What are the most important things in an individual's life? The support of good health, money and wisdom all seem necessary for a balanced life. Yet these three things can be overly emphasized and extended to unrealistic proportions and ambition.

If an individual could not attain all of them, which one should be eliminated? The answer for some would be to eliminate wisdom. They believe that wisdom is a luxury. So, after removing wisdom, there are two left. If a person could not have both health and wealth at the same time, which one should be given up? The answer would be different according to the life experience of the person answering. A young or inexperienced person might say, "I would like to have lots of money. If I become ill, I could pay many good doctors and beautiful nurses to take care of me. Wealth is what I need." Another person, one who has attained some growth, would probably say, "I would like to have health. I could enjoy that throughout my lifetime, and having it would enable me to make my own money."

From these two different answers, you can see that the growth from one's life experience makes each individual's understanding of life different. This necessary growth is called wisdom. If there is no wisdom, a person cannot use his money correctly or maintain his wealth. Without wisdom, a person cannot maintain the health with which nature endowed him. From this understanding, we can see that wisdom is the light of life. A person cannot live enjoyably without it. I am not talking about the wisdom of the great sages who have lived and are remembered and admired by people in later generations. I am promoting the simple wisdom of life. This kind of wisdom is not separate from the essence of daily life, which is the same for a great life and an ordinary one.

This book will explore and reveal the wisdom each of us needs everyday. It takes care of us. It guides us toward right action. This wisdom is not something that any one individual has created. It is an essence preserved within us gathered from millions of years of human evolution; it is the essence of natural life experience. With wisdom, you can improve your health, increase your wealth and expand your wisdom. With the attainment of wisdom, you know how to direct your health and wealth to support your life.

There is no better insurance than wisdom. Wisdom serves you truthfully and directly. It is your own achievement. It is universal and it is natural. This is what I was taught and learned. My parents and forefathers were educated with this when they were young. They made the young ones recite this wisdom so that afterwards in their life experiences, the words would come back into their minds to act as a compass or a guide. Thus, they could avoid spending hours or days in confusion.

Other books might establish and promote an external authority you can go to for help. In this book, I do not tell you that there is any external authority you can go to for help; there is you, yourself. I respect the authority of life within you. Once you extend the energy of your own life authority, your life is complete. You see, in your life, you have learned to take in almost everything from the outside world to support your life, but few people know the secret that your own life energy can be your main support. Once that happens, your life will be complete. That is another illustration of what I call the wisdom of every person and everyday.

Wisdom is not something you can swallow without chewing carefully. If you swallow it whole, it will not be digested, absorbed and be beneficial. Spiritual growth cannot reach the height of six feet in a couple of hours. Anyone who utilizes this book should not be too anxious to sit down in one hour and read the entire book. Well, you might do that, but if you do, then come back to read it over and over again, sentence by sentence, paragraph by paragraph and chapter by chapter. It is known that the best concentration of a person's mind lasts for twenty minutes. After twenty minutes, one's concentration is not as good as when the mind is fresh. So it is helpful to read a little at a time so you can obtain the greatest benefit from it.

This important book will be the manifestation of your personal life. Some of you will discover that you are already in the book and you only need to read through it to re-discover where you are. It is your book. Some of you may find that there is only one part of you that is in this book, so you can use the rest of it to help complete yourself. Those who are already sages but who are humble will find that it is good for them to read it as I recommend: study the whole book thoroughly. To those of you who have the virtue of modesty, I do not suggest that you jump from one page to the next, but read the words and repeat them; remember them as you should.

Most of you will find your counterpart in the developed one or the student of spiritual development. But any way you read this book, it will be a confirmation for your life. It should be easy to recite and useful for an entire lifetime as materials in the *Workbook for Spiritual Development* that is used for your daily cultivation.   Once you remember these lines, anytime you need them in a given situation, the guidance will flow into the mind.   Though the life pattern today is much different from that of the ancient herdsmen or agricultural society, the basics are still the same. People still experience confusion of days or months. Through learning from this book when you have a few minutes, you will later immediately find the light and see the stepping stones in front of you to carry you safely towards your own life goal: health, wealth and wisdom.

The following chapters are the most important fundamental contributions from the ageless teaching of the ancient wise ones; you might find life in them. They also might find life in you.

CHAPTER TWO

Spiritual Realization

"The learning of the subtle integral truth comes through a process of discovering one's self and discovering the truth of life. It requires that a person be aligned in each moment with his spiritual nature.

"It is a great pleasure to be close to friends who have attained knowledge of the subtle natural truth and who have learned to respect each other. One who has this knowledge is not angered by those who do not see the natural truth.

"One who knows to help the less developed is seldom disrespectful or aggressive. One who knows to respect others seldom disturbs the harmony, good order or naturalness in any environment with his personal approach.

"One who attains awareness of spiritual self responsibility knows to take care of the fundamentals of his life; from this basis he promotes progress for the whole of human life by helping the less developed. That is the root of all positive life beings."

"A student of spiritual development should examine himself with these three criteria each day: Am I faithful when I work for people? Am I faithful toward friends by not sacrificing the integral natural truth? Do I align myself, in all aspects of my life, with the integral natural truth that I have learned?"

"To the one who has the opportunity to serve the public: be faithful and respect the work you do. Love and take care of people. Do not waste public money. Use your authority correctly. Guide people properly.

"To the student of the subtle law: respect your parents and love your brothers and sisters. Be prudent in activities without causing harm to yourself or anyone else. Love everyone without partiality and learn from the developed ones. First realize the above, then extend yourself to learn and practice the arts while you still have energy, so you can have correct and healthy fun that does not conflict with your basic fulfillment of life."

"To achieve oneself, if a person could turn the mind away from the insatiable pursuit of physical pleasure towards the learning of the subtle integral truth of spiritual nature, be supportive to one's parents, be dutiful in helping his society, be faithful in keeping one's word and diligent in accomplishing one's deeds; such a person, though he may not have academic degrees, would be considered by me as developed."

"The one who attains awareness of spiritual self responsibility knows to respect himself with what he has attained. He is loyal and faithful in not making close friends who are less than his own character. He is also not afraid of correcting any mistake that he might make."

"To achieve yourself: In your behavior, always consider what will be the result of your speech or actions and what possible effects you will cause. In this way, you assist the well-being of society."

"A junior student asked a senior student of the developed one: 'When a developed one comes to a place, his greatest concern is the well-being of the society. What does he do? Does he comment on it or accept it as it is?'

"The senior student replied, 'The developed one remains himself: kind, non-confronting, respectful of others, effective and modest. Thus, he wins the friendship of the people. What he wants is different from what ordinary people want, so he accepts any society as it is and works in his own way for the well-being of the people.'"

"To achieve oneself: What determines an individual's good life is the direction he chooses for his life when he is young, how he behaves when he is independent, and when there is no external restraint, discipline or other person watching, if he continues to behave responsibly. After considering all three, it can be decided whether or not this individual is on the path of spiritual development."

"To achieve oneself: In making any contact with others, harmony is of the first importance. Harmony should be realized in all relationships and is a sign of spiritual development. However, it is important that you only harmonize with people after you have the knowledge that what they do is virtuous and with good motivation.   This means that we must know that the people we associate with are involved in virtuous activities or work.

"In harmonizing with other people and situations, we need to be aware of the nature or character of what we harmonize with. Otherwise, the harmony is partial

and it would damage the righteousness of the
individual."

"To achieve oneself: If a person makes a mistake
but does not lie and thus takes the blame for it, the
person is still considered to be trustworthy.
"If a person does not behave with refined manners,
but is straightforward and earnest, he is not considered disgraced.
"If a person is natural and kind, although he does
not attain perfection of his being, he is not a disgrace
to his relatives."

"To achieve oneself: A person pursuing spiritual
development does not look for great satisfaction in
eating nor for excessive comfort or luxury in life. He is
serious in his work, frugal in his speech and tries to
cultivate virtue in his inner life. Such a one is a good
student of the integral truth of spiritual nature."

"A student discussed with his teacher: 'If someone
is poor but does not look for special favors, or is rich
but thinks he is not particularly important, can this
person be a good student of the Integral Truth?'
"The teacher replied, 'It is even better for a person
when poor not to damage his happy nature, and to
demonstrate great modesty when he achieves success.'

"The student said: 'That can only be produced by
spiritual self-inspection.'
"The teacher answered, 'You know the source of
spiritual progress.'"

"In achieving yourself: It is not a problem when people do not know your greatness but they only know your shortcomings. It is a problem when you do not know people's greatness and you do not know your own shortcomings."

CHAPTER THREE

You Are in the Light

"To achieve oneself, the function of spiritual culti-vation is similar to seeing the North Star in the dark of night. It is surrounded by all the other stars - in other words, it is surrounded by all different aspects of life - and yet it brings about orderliness and light out of any possible confusion."

"To achieve oneself, one realizes that all spiritual customs and religious practices were developed by races and tribes in different ways at different times. Yet, in all the different rituals, there is the same essence. It is through any of these formalities that one's spiritual sincerity and purity is exercised and expressed.
"The specifics or details of different formalities are not crucial; it is the spiritual essence of each individu-al that is paramount."

"It is achievement to know that by directing people with rigid governmental regulations and laws, in order to avoid the punishment of the government, people will behave according to the laws.
"By directing people with spiritual development, however, the people will keep correcting and refining themselves without need of external authority."

"To achieve oneself, an individual at age 15 should set up his own goals for spiritual development and start disciplining himself without the need of being watched. At 30, he needs to improve his independent judgement. At 40, he needs to eliminate self-doubt and totally accept his duty in life. At 50, he should give up personal struggling with his own spiritual nature and can detach from the world. At 60, he should not be confused by anything of the world any more. After 70, he should be able to do whatever and go wherever without causing damage to his or anyone else's health."

"A developed one was asked a question about how to travel on the path of life. The answer he gave was: 'Do nothing against your nature.'
"The question was furthered: 'How?'
"Came the reply, 'When active, do nothing against your spiritual nature; be harmonious with your nature. When dying, do nothing against your nature. When your life continues, whenever and whatever, still do nothing against your spiritual nature."

"The same question was asked by another student. The answer was, 'Do nothing to cause trouble or confusion to yourself or others.'"

"The question of how to travel on the path of life was asked again. The response was, 'People think that the purpose of living is to provide themselves with all good things. Living thus is no different than living the life of a beast. What is superior about a life with spiritual awareness is living with a greater purpose of realizing spiritual harmony within and without.'"

"The same question was brought by another student. A developed one answered: 'Doing nothing against the subtle law of nature is to follow the law of life. It is the spiritual law of all souls. Thus, do whatever job you need to do; that will be a benefit you can share with others.'"

"A good student of spiritual development is not one who learns to talk well, but one who would rather be quietly learning and working. With quietude there comes internal inspection, which provides even greater attainment.

"'A person cannot hide. By whatever he does, the true facts about him can be known. Thus, it is important to be sincere in life.

"'In studying the truth, review what you have learned. Apply it to your life. Then see if new experiences emerge that reflect increased success. New experiences can be your greatest teachers.

"'To become achieved, a developed person does not narrow himself by overextending his personal interests nor diminish himself by doing what is not considered respectable.'"

"'What is a developed person?' a student asked. The wise one answered, 'A developed person is one who manifests his honest nature directly in his life, but this is not done by using lofty conceptions or words.

"'A developed person is one who loves all people universally. An underdeveloped person is one who attracts people only for selfish reasons.'"

"A good student is one who knows that learning without examining what he is learning will lead to being falsely knowledgeable.   On the other hand, thinking and ruminating within oneself without learning from the outside world will lead one into a blind alley.

"Spiritual learning rests on the simple common human foundation on which all the colorful religions and cultures are based.   It is harmful to neglect this foundation in favor of exalted customs and conceptions of religions and cultures.

"The achieved student is the one who is honest about what he knows and what he does not know. This understanding is his first attainment."

"A young ambitious person who was pursuing social glory received guidance from a developed one: 'Extend your knowledge to all and remain unassertive about the subtle facts that have not been truly seen. Save yourself from disgrace by not talking about things you really do not yet know anything about.   Speak no regretful words and make no remorseful actions. One's social glory lies therein.'

"He asked, 'How will I make people agree with me?'

"The developed one said, 'Agree with what is universally right for people and disapprove of what is universally not right for people.   People will finally agree with you and support you.'

"'How can I make people happy with their lives and have respect for society?'

"'The leaders of a society must not steal or twist the will of the people, but faithfully move in the direction of the common good.   Those who are wise and capable should be leaders, and those who are faithful and able should be the workers.'

"'Is political administration different from individual life?'

"'No. Good government starts in an individual's personal life and extends to his family. When fairness, justice, righteousness and mutual assistance are nurtured within the foundation of family, it naturally extends to the rest of the world.'

"'An untrustworthy government is like an automobile whose front wheels are out of balance and alignment. The people's will and the government's will go against each other. Such a government, like the automobile, must fail.

"'One who obeys a powerful but unrighteous leader is engaging in evil flattery; it eventually harms both the leader and oneself. Seeing what is unrighteous, but not confronting and correcting it is the sign of a real coward.'

"'Can the future of a society be known?'

"'Yes. The future is decided by the present. Today's serious sickness damages the future health of an individual life. Darkness and prejudice in leadership damage the future of a healthy society.'"

CHAPTER FOUR

Essence is Simple

"Developed people do not support corrupt leadership or a government that indulges itself in spending and expansion. Instead, they work to alleviate suffering."

"If a person is not kind, even if he has many social graces, he is underdeveloped."

"'What is the basic principle of social ceremony?' asked a student.

"'The basic principle when conducting a personal or social ceremony is that the activity should be meaningful, but not wasteful of material goods. Waste can aggravate emotional instability and encourage bad personal habits.'"

"All undeveloped groups of people enjoy having a dependable ruler. Practicing self-government is more self-responsible than having a ruler with concentrated authority."

"In situations of rivalry, contest or competition, a developed person learns and displays self-control and good manners. In situations where something attractive appeals to him, a developed person again learns and displays self-control and good manners, whether it be in public or private."

"The example of good conduct should be given by the developed ones."

"Exercising one's sincerity in daily circumstances is more important than displaying it only on special occasions of prayer or when making an offering. Actually, the most important element of prayer or offering is an individual's spiritual sincerity.   An individual's sincerity in any circumstance of life is direct communication with the spiritual nature of the universe.   This sincerity is lost if a person tries to assign responsibility for his life to an external authority."

"The frequent displaying of grand ceremonies is not as essential as leading of a simple, truthful life."

"One's true gain in learning martial arts is the improved concentration, effective movement and coordination of body and mind that comes with the added benefit of health and personal control.   It is not in learning to become a great fighter."

"Being polite is a sign of refinement of a personality, while scheming or flattery is a sign of loss of personal dignity."

"A question was presented to a developed one: 'How does a superior command his subordinates and how do subordinates work with their superior?'

"It was answered: 'The superior commands his subordinates with love and politeness. Subordinates work for their superior with all dutifulness and truthfulness.'"

"A developed person enjoys all things, but none to excess. A developed person also can be frustrated by circumstances, but he does not allow that frustration to damage the nature of his internal harmony."

"A developed person does not demand explanations for what was done by others. He gives no advice about what has already been accomplished and does not seek accountability from others for their past errors. He watches what comes from himself. This means he keeps his focus within and does not blame or make others responsible for problems in his life."

"Good music leads to internal harmony and joy; it helps restore a harmonious internal order. Music thus helps develop a harmonious personality. It helps one regain personal health. Good music has spiritual value."

"Good music must be produced from a harmonious personality. It influences social behavior and affects individual and group emotion. Thus, the selection of music for individual or social use expresses the level of development of the people who choose it."

"The holy path of spiritual development cannot be lost as long as the awakening truth is voiced through a developed one."

CHAPTER FIVE

Internal Strength

"When you choose a community in which to live or people to be your companions, look for people who are kind, loving and wise. By so doing, you will receive inspiration and develop wisdom."

"Those who are unkind will not live in peace in any life situation.
"Only those of kindness and love are self-contented and contained.
"Only those of wisdom are creative in loving each other."

"Only those of kindness and love are decisive enough to support others of kindness and love, and withdraw support from those unkind and prejudicial."

"A person with the intention of good will must be a kind person."

"Becoming rich and noble is what all people desire; but if wealth is not gained correctly, it is not truly beneficial for them.
"Being poor and feeling inferior is what most people dislike. But if developed ones do not have an opportunity to improve their lives with a correct approach, they would rather remain by themselves in serenity, living righteously and working on strengthening themselves."

"If a person is not kind and wise, he cannot become developed. By finding one's kind and righteous being and not separating from it, one becomes developed."

"He who dislikes evil doing must create what is right for himself and not allow evil to be done to him. If a situation is out of control, he should become more watchful in the future. He should not dwell on the suffering caused by the evildoing of someone else or himself."

"He who decides to be kind and loving is always powerful and never lacks strength."

"In a group effort, if an error is committed, it should be seen and corrected by someone in the group. That is better than someone outside the group catching the error. The one in the group who sees the mistake is the developed one."

"The ambition of the developed one is to embody the light of truth in his life. He has no regrets even if he dies the night after the day he has successfully fulfilled and embodied his life with the truth."

"A student aspiring to attain truth is not ashamed if he has to live in material difficulty."

"The developed one who lives under Heaven associates with no one in the low and unvirtuous part of worldly life."

"Developed people care about good; so when taking action, their mind always asks, 'What harm might possibly be brought about by this behavior to myself and other people?'
"Undeveloped people care about comfort, so when taking action, their mind always asks, 'What favor will I gain through this behavior for myself?'"

"The path of spiritual development requires persistence. When working for one's own benefit, always be sure that no one will suffer from it."

"The developed one has as his goal righteousness even when he takes a profit. The undeveloped has profit as his goal, and that is all he can see."

"To achieve oneself, acknowledge the developed ones and wish to be like them. See the undeveloped ones and inspect yourself."

"When a person is in public service, he offers his advice. If his personal idea is not accepted, he should not lose the respect and cooperation of society or turn against society. It takes a long time for a people to know what is right. This means we are all in the process of learning and we need to have patience with each other.

"A developed one is not afraid of isolation if he knows he is correct and this is not accepted by others. However, a person who is right always finds supportive friends."

"A developed one does not frequently comment on nor attack his society for its small wrongs. He does not comment on nor attack his friends for their small mistakes."

"Exclusively holding the goal of personal profit brings about conflict."

"Righteousness cannot exist together with evil competition. A system that restrains evil competition brings about a healthy society. Evil competition is characterized by immoral or underhanded actions. Healthy competition, on the other hand, is honest and moral.

"A healthy society will lessen political contention. Self-government is the only true civilization among humans; it must be protected by all people."

"Social position is not important. What is important is the place in which you now stand."

"Do not worry if others do not know your capability, but work on preparing yourself sufficiently to perform your tasks."

"Apply a cautious mind to know the trends of your society. This is helpful to be open to the improvement of its well being and to resist its pressures for evil development."

"A developed one does not easily abandon his homeland; there must be a correct reason to leave one's society."

"When the world is suffering a downfall, a developed one does not speak unless he follows it up with appropriate action on the world's behalf."

"The developed one speaks effectively, moves effectively and spends effectively."

"A developed one does not merely speak words, he is swift in action."

CHAPTER SIX

A Good Character
Is True Gold

"A developed one recognizes a person's true character. He will even permit his daughter to marry a true gentleman whose reputation suffers from misunderstanding."

"A developed one lives well in a properly governed society, yet can live far away from the unjust persecution of a poorly governed society. Such a man can raise a family."

"A developed one finds true teachers by keeping good company and living with those who develop themselves spiritually. He learns from their example and influence."

"It is important for all young people to cultivate their personalities and develop themselves to be useful and helpful to the world. Those young people will not starve."

"A sweet tongue does not make a person trustworthy. An individual earns the trust of others by his character."

"In serving the public and in attending to personal affairs, it is not good to be overly self-confident. A person of openness is a person who manages or handles his work with prudence."

"A developed one would rather take a boat to travel on the seas if his advice is not accepted by the people. He would not start a war to force people to follow him."

"People's talents are different. Some can administer the national revenue and others can be governors or diplomats. Though their tasks may be different, their character of public mindedness must be equally sound."

"Some people can know ten things from hearing one thing. Some people can know two things from hearing one. It is not shameful to know something through learning one thing. It is no shame to have a slow mind; it is a shame not to improve it."

"Rotten wood cannot be used for building. Muddy soil does not make good bricks. Anyone who allows himself to be rotten and his life to be purposeless like muddy soil will not find the true use of life."

"It is childish to trust a person only by hearing his words. It is better to observe his conduct and then listen to his speech."

"A truly powerful leader is one who has no personal interest or desire."

"Do not do something to others that you would not like them to do to you."

"From people's writings and speeches, their spiritual achievement can be known. What about people who have no writings and give no speeches? Their spiritual achievement can be known from their life and work."

"It is not difficult to accumulate great quantities of knowledge from many great teachers. What is difficult is to practice that knowledge in one's life. One who is too enthusiastic in the pursuit of much knowledge may obstruct his own realization of even a small amount of it."

"A civilized person does not necessarily hold high academic degrees. He can be known by his politeness, desire to learn and acceptance of his natural limitations. This is being civilized."

"A good leader has four traits: self-respect, respect for his duty, helpfulness to all people and proper use of the authority entrusted in him."

"A good friend is the one who earns your respect over a long time."

"A person who devotes himself to public service never lives an overly luxurious life."

"A person of true public mindedness is not over-joyed when receiving a high position in society. He does not feel unhappy when he is put in an ordinary position. Either place, his purpose is to serve other people."

"A wise person never cooperates with an unjust government, and if necessary, will move away from it. The highly developed one, however, would find a way to improve such a society."

"People think a matter over many times before acting upon it; this is not effective. Too much thinking leads to indecision and often misses the opportunity that has been presented."

"Balanced thinking perceives the good and the bad, the pros and the cons of a situation.
"Thinking that sees only one side of a matter is distorted and imbalanced."

"When a society is well ordered, people can express their capabilities to assist it. When a society is con-fused and the unrighteous rule the righteous, it is time to keep to oneself.
"It is not hard to display one's talent; it is hard to display one's talent during a time of evil leadership."

"It is best to help the development of young ones when one's ambition of an orderly world cannot be fulfilled. This means that when the social order is corrupt, it is best to put one's energy into helping the young."

"Do not seek revenge if someone has violated you in the past. If they have changed and are in a different stage of life in the present, you would be putting old hatred onto a new person."

"Offer help from yourself. Do not borrow someone else's help to give to another; that is not truly upright. Yet in public service, it is always right to use society to help society."

"Appreciate it when someone is polite and friendly to you. However, it is hypocritical to go along with someone you resent until your complaint is cleared up."

"For all to have a great spiritual achievement is a good ambition."

"It is fine for a person to have the ambition to obtain positive things so that he may share with friends without reservation. It is also fine for a person to achieve himself in all ways, including spiritually, but not for the purpose of showing off to others. A person of spiritual achievement does not look for attention from other people."

"Achieving the world means to live a life which is harmonious with all people. It is enjoying the trust people give to you. It is helping the old people have a pleasant and peaceful life, and giving all the young ones a good opportunity to grow correctly and healthily."

"It is rare to see a person admit a mistake he has made without defending himself for his responsibility."

"In any small community, there must always be someone who is nice and kind. It is rare to see the nice and kind one become the leader or ruler."

CHAPTER SEVEN

Govern Complication with Simplicity

"The capability and great talent of a leader is to govern complication with simplicity while respecting the important details. A person with such talent is truly helpful in his duty."

"A good student of spiritual development does not transfer his anger to someone else after he has made a mistake, suffers frustration from an unachieved plan or is criticized by someone. In his personal behavior, he does not commit the same mistake twice."

"Regarding helping another person with his or her needs, a student of spiritual development would rather help someone who is in a state of emergency than make a flattering gift to someone who is rich."

"The developed one does not treat a person with ill manners because of low birth or because of the character of his parents."

"A good student of spiritual development never takes his mind away from his spiritual development."

"Anyone who is decisive, has good understanding and is capable would be wise to bring forward his qualities to benefit the public."

"A student of spiritual development would refuse a position under a corrupted leader. He would also refuse a position that would enable himself to receive benefit from a corrupted group."

"A good student of spiritual development does not burden others with his excuses."

"A good student of spiritual development is not ashamed to live a simple and humble material life when the time is not right for him to receive abundant material support."

"A good student of spiritual development will not stop halfway, but proceeds to the higher goals of endless spiritual development."

"To live is to learn and to attain spiritual development. Those who refuse their own spiritual development cheat themselves."

"A respectable person does things in an upright way without trying to please one's superiors. Such behavior is truly respectful."

"A respectful person is like the example of the person riding with a defeated army. While all the other riders whip their horses to speed up their fleeing, a respectful one intentionally guards the re-treating troops by slowing his horse. Afterwards, he also refuses credit for his good deed by saying, 'My horse would not run fast.'"

"Those who are good in words and have an attractive appearance easily become popular. Yet, those who are silent and hard workers are more respectable."

"Whenever somebody enters or leaves a house, he must go through a door. The path of spiritual development is like going through a doorway. When somebody enters life or exits from life, he needs to go through the door of life."

"If a person expresses his originality more than he follows the social code of manners, he is considered uncivilized. However, usually a good reputation is earned by one whose social manners cover his originality. Therefore, it is valuable to maintain one's originality and at the same time, to work with social manners."

"All people are straight when they are born. Being straight is necessary but is accepted by very few. Even fewer people can keep their spiritual naturalness.

"Most people can keep their physical life alive long after their straight quality and originalness has died. People who have a twisted mind do not see that they have been dying for a long time."

"In life, it takes a long time to attain wide knowledge and become proud of it. It is better, however, to learn something that one can enjoy and benefit during one's whole lifetime. That something is to cultivate, maintain and continually refine the good qualities you were born with."

"With people above the general level, one can talk about something high and subtle. With other people, the high and subtle things cannot be accepted and trusted. Such a task must be done by good teachers, because it is the general people who also contain high potential and need development."

"People of wisdom respect the unadorned truth of oneness as the spiritual reality of nature.

"In making friends, people of wisdom do not foolishly insist on any human spiritual custom which was established as a religion. It is hard to become spiritually developed from the influence of unnatural boundaries. However, it is possible for a person to successfully go through conceptual walls and befriend all people.

"Living a life of spiritual development means to accept what is difficult when others look for what is easy. It means not to enjoy personal happiness until all people can be in harmony.

To achieve oneself, a person is concerned with the world until the people of the entire world start to recognize the mistakes they have not seen. He can be happy only when the people of the world are friendly and are overcoming their troubles."

"Wisdom is similar to the energy of flowing water. Kindness and independence are similar to the energy of a tall mountain. Therefore, the wise one enjoys water energy. The kind one enjoys mountain energy. The one who enjoys water energy likes activity in a creative and effective way. The one who enjoys mountain energy likes to remain quiet and independent.

"Happiness belongs to the wise who like to stay with oceans far away from the competitive world. They are happy with water and beneficial activities.

"Longevity and independence are the enjoyment of the kind who keep company with the high and rural mountains. They like to remain quiet without causing people trouble. They are happy with the mountains."

"The worth of a strong nation is to be a reliable worldly friend which gives help but is not aggressive. The worth of an upright person is to live a life with no spiritual boundary and give help to all the developed ones."

"Battles, battles carry all talent away."

"A spiritually developed person is the one who, when told someone fell into a deep well, would find a way to help from the top of the well. He would not jump into the well in order to display his kindness.

"He might be deceived by someone on occasion, but he does not offer himself through a negative sacrifice."

"A developed one can be well versed in the rules of the human game, but he would not utilize such knowledge to seek personal gain. His understanding of the game rules enables him to maintain his independence without causing friction with other people."

"A developed person is not afraid of being misunderstood by others because he meets with a person of bad reputation who seeks his advice. Even if he disapproves of the person's behavior and character, he still offers an opportunity for the lost person to receive his good influence and help."

"Centeredness in one's personal behavior is achievable by people. Yet people cannot keep it long without again running into extremes. This motion is similar to that of a large society suffering through historical steps of extreme times."

"Being charitable to all people when one is able to do so is holy. In cases when one's supportive strength is low and great charity cannot be made, it is better to expand one's personal spiritual cultivation to help whomever is in need. When a person expands his energy to help people, he is helped too at the same time."

CHAPTER EIGHT

Quiet Observation Gains the Most

"A spiritually developed teacher has learned the spiritual truth and would like to impart it to his students. He does not become personal or self-opinionated in giving what he has learned."

"A spiritually developed teacher is achieved by keeping himself in quiet observation and constantly working towards reaching correct understanding. He never tires of giving help to young people; doing this increases his confirmation in making further progress.

"Quiet observation, constantly working to reach correct understanding and being untiring in helping others all build up the worthiness of a person. The person thus receives the benefit of refreshing the learning experiences for further development."

"A spiritually developed teacher is self-contented and happy in his personal life."

"A student of spiritual development always holds the vision of the spiritual goal and model he is going to fulfill."

"To a spiritually developed person, harmony with his innate spiritual nature is his basic foundation, loving people is his principle and enjoyment of all refining arts is his interest."

"A spiritually developed teacher is sincere to all those who come to him with large or small gifts, or a significant token, in recognition of him as their teacher.

"A teacher can always advise a student and a student can serve a teacher."   Note: in today's commercial world, I think instruction can be given in classes of a reasonable charge, and the relationship between teacher and student can be as friends according to the modern social code.

"A good student of spiritual development knows that where there is no challenge, there is no enlightenment, and where there is no stimulation, there is no understanding.

"A teacher only teaches one aspect of a thing and lets the student develop his own understanding of the rest.   The teacher always provides an opportunity for a student to develop his own mind.   He does not grow for his students instead of letting his students grow by themselves.   The teacher only offers direction for a student's development."

"A developed one does not enjoy his food when somebody is suffering with sadness nearby."

"A developed one does not sing when someone has sorrow at his side."

"A developed one can exercise his talent to do a thing well in response to the request of authority.   He can keep himself detached when he is not thought to be the choice."

"A spiritually developed strategy of commanding military strength does not depend on force or brutal courage to accomplish the mission. He avoids confrontation and finds the best and most successful way to win the victory for both sides without war."

"A spiritually developed person would do what is upright and makes him happy, not what is disgraceful that could make him rich."

"A spiritually developed person avoids the following three things: participating in religious ritual or sacrifice, causing or going to war, and anything that brings about sickness."

"A spiritually developed person finds that meat is not essential to his diet, and good music assists the balance and harmony of his emotion."

"A spiritually developed one does not help people establish their evil competitive aims. He respects the one who practices yielding an opportunity to someone else with no complaint."

"A spiritually developed one can be happy with a simple life and simple food. He does not enjoy richness or power taken by unrighteous means."

"A spiritually developed one, as he grows older, becomes increasingly better versed in the principles from the *Book of Changes and the Unchanging Truth* so that his life will have fewer mistakes and so he will attain embodiment of the subtle law."

"A spiritually developed person uses good language in his public contacts and private life."

"A student who aspires to spiritual development may be so engrossed with his learning that he forgets eating, and is so happy with what he is doing, he forgets his troubles. He may not notice old age approaching him because of his spiritual pursuit."

"A spiritually developed one is not someone who is born with all beneficial knowledge, but he likes useful knowledge and is diligent in learning."

"A spiritually developed one does not promote things that are strange, forceful, confusing or disordering, such as groundless stories of ghosts, spirits or image of a powerful monster to be the God or master of the world."

"A student of spiritual development is the one who knows that in any group of three, there will be someone or something that will be his teacher. He continues to learn in each situation and corrects what is wrong in his behavior from watching the good example of others."

"After contemplating the subtle law, a developed one yields in matters involving material struggle, even if he sees a good opportunity for making a profit. He would rather yield or negotiate by arbitration to restore peace. This is in the best interests of everyone.

"After contemplating the subtle law, if one knows he is wrong spiritually, even when tempted by material profit and gain, he will not exchange his righteousness for his private interests.

"After contemplating the subtle law, if one knows that what he is doing or saying is right for all people but that his words or actions will cause him unfavorably to face a situation of misunderstanding as personal challenge and danger, he will still not trade his great righteousness to gain his personal safety."

"A spiritually developed person hides nothing from his close friend or companion. His conduct and personal behavior is witnessed by all."

"A teacher of spiritual development would teach four things: spiritual teachings from the ancient developed ones, the realization of that spiritual heritage, being loyal to one's own honest nature and being faithful in doing all things."

"A student of spiritual development does not strive to meet a person of special achievement whom he holds up as an idol in his imagination. He is satisfied to see ordinary and upright people in his daily contacts."

"A student of spiritual development does not wait to meet a more virtuous person before improving himself. The truthful way to realize one's spiritual nature is to live a life cultivating natural qualities such as persistence, honesty, earnestness and sincerity. To be as natural as one can be, without resorting to artificial religious reasons for doing and being good, is his best model.

"When the false civilization arises, people pretend to be what they are not. This is the result of the promotion of false standards. That is the time when the spiritually unachieved teach how to achieve, the unlearned teach how to become learned and the sick-minded ones are taken for healthy. The positions of leadership in society are seized by people who are not really what they say they are."

"A leader who has attained spiritual development does not use his power to persecute innocent people who might be related to the real troublemaker. Also, a spiritually developed one does not fight his opponent by means of secret schemes."

"A spiritually developed teacher does not teach what he does not know or what has not been experienced by him. He chooses the right thing from among the many things he has learned, worked with and benefitted from.

"One who discovers useful knowledge has attained high wisdom. It is great. In later generations, it is also great when someone chooses to teach the spiritual discoveries of previous teachers. He must have a spiritual quality equal to those who came before; he is able to rediscover the value of truth."

"A spiritually developed teacher does not refuse to meet a person with a misguided background, because that person may be asking for help in attempting to step out of his past mistakes. Improvement could be the result of the meeting."

"Is the attainment of spiritual development difficult? Simply by deciding to seek spiritual learning, a person has made progress."

"A spiritually developed one does not cover up the mistakes of his relatives, friends or countrymen. A spiritually developed one does not cover his own mistakes; he admits them."

"A spiritually developed one does not take pride in what he says. He admires what he does to improve himself."

"A spiritually developed one never accepts himself as having reached sageliness nor complete development. He admits only to not being tired of doing it and teaching it."

"It is not when a spiritually developed one is sick or troubled that he repents and prays; he does it constantly by living a positive life."

"A spiritually developed one knows that luxury is not moderation. Being moderate is what makes him strong and firm in character. He would rather be firm in his character than become extravagant."

"The spiritually developed one is easily contented and not picky in his life, while the undeveloped one keeps endlessly struggling for his personal ends. He carries worry at all times because he does not know it is life which sustains life. It is not worry which works to sustain life."

"A spiritually developed teacher is a person of warmth and strictness. He is powerful but gentle. He is authoritative but not pompous. He is calm and respecting."

CHAPTER NINE

High Virtue is not Noticeable

"The highly spiritually developed one knows to yield an opportunity to someone who is more suitable for an authoritative position. He walks away from competition and never turns back to it. People may forget him. He does not want people to remember him as a threat."

"People may be respectful, prudent, courageous and straight, but without spiritual development to attain insight and control, those positive traits would change into negative ones. Politeness would turn into ineffectiveness, prudence into indecision, bravery into impulsiveness and straightforwardness into aggression."

"A spiritually developed person is one who can love all people as he loves his parents."

"When a teacher who had attained spiritual development was on his deathbed, he told his students, 'Please raise the blankets and look to see that my hands and feet are still there. It is my pride. Through my lifetime, I have kept them intact and safe, without damaging them by not living morally or by causing legal problems. (Note: In one stage of ancient customs, around 2,500 years ago, some small kingdoms would punish a thief by having his hands or feet cut off. This was discontinued in the Han Dynasty. Yet, the punishment reappeared in the Middle East in the

Islamic culture.) All of you, remember to respect your body and limbs as I do and do not damage them in your life. In this moment, I am glad I have protected them well without allowing my desires to cut them off or hurt them. This is the last advice I give to you.'"

"A spiritually developed one was about to pass away, and a person of high position requested that he give some teachings. He replied, 'When a bird is going to die, its song becomes sad. When a human is going to die, his words become truthful. A person of responsibility should live his life like someone walking on the edge of a high cliff, traveling over a road at the side of an unfathomable abyss or moving over thin ice on the winter river. Each step must be carefully taken in order to avoid making a mistake in one's life.'"

"He continued teaching: 'Spiritual practice grooms people. It polishes rough and careless manners, allows one's face to radiate the vibration of uprightness and faithfulness from its depths, and makes language convey truthful reason. Learning the procedures of superficial ritual is not as important as this basic training.'"

"A spiritually developed one does not think other people are less learned than himself. He never thinks he is full of all knowledge. He does not feel offended when facing a challenge."

"When a person like a soldier of a defensive army is assigned to protect the young or support the weak, he totally understands it is out of righteous reason. Thus, when there is a danger for him in fulfilling his duty, he will not choose his personal safety over his duty. Similarly, in any situation, no threat or profit can make him change when he knows what is right to do. He must be very firm. The person who has attained spiritual development is able to do this."

"The person attaining spiritual development must have far reaching ambition and persistent strength. He takes the spiritual development of mankind as his spiritual duty. He has undaunted courage to carry on with it during all his lifetimes. He is not afraid his journey will be long."

"A person of spiritual development made his three wishes: Let my life flow like a natural lyric, let my strength be under self-control and let my life be accomplished like a piece of peaceful music."

"All people need trustworthy guidance. If they become negative and destructive, it is because the guidance they have chosen is wrong. It is the responsibility of the spiritually developed one to find the appropriate guidance from the principles of balance which can be found in the *Book of Changes and the Unchanging Truth.*"

"The one who tends to act impulsively and hates living in poverty will create trouble. The one who identifies himself as bad is capable of hurting others. Spiritual development must be taught to all people."

"A person of talent loses his worth if he is proud and stingy in giving help to others."

"After some time, people wish to transform all their learning and development into money. Those who take time and use energy for true learning and for receiving the true reward are rare."

"A spiritually developed one is sincere in learning and insists on an upright path. He offers his talents when the world is right.

"He will not stay in a troubled or incorrectly ordered society. He becomes a hermit in an ordinary job when the world loses its healthy direction. It is a shame when such a person is poor and cannot use his talents, but it would be a greater shame for him to accept the money and position of a confused leadership. He does not accept a position which is not right for him and he is not endowed with the power to correct wrong doing."

"Living in a healthy society is like the enjoyment of grand music."

"Even a highly developed teacher is unable to help a person who is thought to be out of his mind and is not honest, a person who is uneducated but who likes to theorize on all matters in his surroundings, and a person who is capable of telling artful lies."

"A student of spiritual development is studious so he does not lose his opportunity for spiritual growth."

"If the leadership of the world is achieved through war or evil competition, those leaders do not earn the respect and cooperation of the spiritually developed leaders."

"The truly great leadership of the world takes as its example the impartial Heaven. It does not dominate. It lets people be natural and free. It does not take credit for being the strength. How great is its success-ful protection. How beautiful is its good example."

"The good leadership of a healthy world needs the participation of truly talented people and the support of all people. It does not need to be the ruler of the entire world; it can be fulfilled by a non-competitive, independent country."

"The good leaders of the world do not pay attention to how well they eat, how beautifully they dress and how grandly they live. They always work for the im-provement of the people's lives."

CHAPTER TEN

Value the Real Life Being

"A spiritually developed person seldom describes to another his profit, his destiny or his spiritual development."

"A spiritually developed person does not take pride in his vast and profound knowledge. He is happy to be versed in simple, everyday work such as cleaning his own place, cooking or driving a car."

"If a spiritually developed one lives in the world, he can follow what most people do if those things are not harmful to his nature. He does not go along with people or do things that are harmful to his sense of righteousness and propriety."

"A spiritually developed one does not hold personal opinion, insist that something must be done, insist on the way something is to be done and persist in doing things his way. In other words, the four things he avoids are: 'It must be me,' 'It is a must,' 'It is necessary,' and 'It is absolutely,' when he applies his mind to the thought of general secondary level activities."

"When a spiritually developed person faces a misunderstanding, he keeps the conviction that, 'the work of spiritual development is the spiritual awakening of oneself. The past great ones have given the example, and the future great ones must continue it.' If he is put into difficulty, such as a situation involving possible loss of his life, he knows it does not mean spiritual development will stop in the world. The difficulty cannot destroy his real life being."

"A spiritually developed one has the capacity to do many things, not because any heavenly gift makes him more versatile nor because he is provided with basic support during his growth. He, like others, must learn and work through much in his life. He is, therefore, vastly knowledgeable, versatile, capable and wise. He does not stop progressing while his life proceeds."

"A spiritually developed one is not necessarily the one who knows all. His response to people who are in doubt and ask questions is to search with them to discover the obstacle that they cannot see by themselves."

"A spiritually developed one knows to fulfill his duty during his lifetime. He does not keep the expectation that a great time of outstanding leaders and a very supportive world will come for him."

"A spiritually developed person makes no disturbance if he sees people at a ceremony or sees mourners. He gives help when he sees the blind or disabled on the roadside."

"A spiritually developed person does not wish people to feel that he is too high to be reached, too deep to exhaust or too great to define. He merely lives up to his nature."

"In instructing a student, a teacher of spiritual development uses the knowledge he has attained to help a student widen his own vision. He guides a student to focus on his own self-improvement, thus the learning is never exhausted. The teacher provides the good advice for starting any stage of life; there is no end to self-progress. Such achievement cannot be expressed by a certificate in a frame."

"A spiritually developed one does not struggle for more and more things. He accepts what comes naturally by itself in a plain life by honest means. He stands on solid ground wherever he is. He does not mean to attract a big group of followers; superficial expansion would bring shame. He would not demand a big funeral at his death either."

"A spiritually developed one does not think of himself as a big piece of beautiful jade kept in safety waiting for a good price to be sold. He offers his help in the right situation without thinking of any reward."

"A spiritually developed one can live in an uncivilized place with ignorant people that may not feel right to him. Wherever he lives, his spiritual development does not stop."

"A spiritually developed one is the one who does not necessarily need people to accept him as a great person, put him in a high position or look to him as a great teacher. He enjoys poems, songs, music, dramas, fine arts and whatever work can enrich people's life and help the health of the world."

"A spiritually developed person can put himself right and do what is necessary in any circumstance to serve a public office, help family members or conduct a meaningful gathering or ceremony. He never becomes incompetent through alcohol or drugs."

"A spiritually developed one keeps moving forward in his life with a positive attitude. He does not allow any negative mistake or habit to stagnate the flow of life. He takes as an example the incessant flow of water in rivers and streams."

"A spiritually developed one loves the improvement of personal character more than the ecstacy of any extremely wonderful sexual opportunity."

"A spiritually developed one is not afraid of doing a big task by making small steps in designated periods of time. He is afraid of stopping and withdrawing any part of his strength and effort towards furthering the progress."

"A student of spiritual development is not lazy about fulfilling a task after being told only once."

"A student of spiritual development is never seen to stop making progress."

"A student of spiritual development never stops mid-way. He sees things through to completion, like crops to the harvest."

"The student of spiritual development is not afraid that someone will achieve higher than he, because he knows that he is not limited by what he is today. He does not fear being old without having a respectable name. He carefully prevents big mistakes before the lid of his coffin is closed."

"Even a strong army commander can be removed from his post. A spiritually developed one, however, holds firmly to his correct goal."

"A student of spiritual development feels no shame if not wearing the fancy clothes of social fashion. He does feel shame when his level of development or right-eousness is inferior to that of other people."

"A student of spiritual development remains harm-less to all and does not engage in the pursuit of evil ends. He is comfortable being with any person. He never thinks his achievement is adequate."

"In the summertime, all trees are lush in the forest; but in the winter, only the pines and cypress are still green. Such persistence belongs to those who have attained the most firm virtues and a firm character in the times of most difficulty."

"The wise one is never confused, the spiritually developed one is never worried about things and the brave one is never afraid."

"It is precious to find someone who has good spiritual development. It is still better that there are many people who have a goal of spiritual development.

"It is marvelous when many people have the goal of spiritual development. It is still better when they work to make what they have achieved available to help other people.

"It is wonderful to see the achieved ones working to help others. It is still better when what is achieved is applied in a way that they remain flexible enough to meet real life situations without becoming rigid. All the past mistakes of dogmatic teaching in dead frameworks of old thought should not be repeated."

"A student of spiritual development is not the one who keeps thinking of seeing beautiful flowers in the Sahara Desert. He works on his internal fragrance and beauty."

"When you are able to see what the good virtues of life actually are, approach them in order to include that goodness in your life. When you are able to distinguish what is harmful or bad, feel you are warned and exclude that harm to yourself or stop doing that inappropriate action in your life. In consequence, you will become so happy by being good.

"On the other hand, one would become unhappy with oneself and dislike oneself by accumulating what is bad or harmful. This proves the truth that you can either bless yourself or curse your own life, filling it with disasters and troubles."

"Someone who is your teacher is a person who can truthfully tell you that you are wrong. A friend is someone who can tell you that you are right and what he says is truthful. A thief is someone who flatters you all the time by telling you that you are right untruthfully and unfaithfully."

"By doing good and being good, you may not see what progress you have made. However, you make a healthy life by reaching what is good and taking advice as warning."

"The value of your life is not decided by your parents; they tend to overly exalt it. It is not decided by someone who dislikes you; he tends to devalue it. The value of all life is the same to nature, yet it can be noticed by you in the things you do everyday that return to you the great strength of a happy and fresh life."

CHAPTER ELEVEN

Lord Over Yourself

"A spiritually developed one is gentle and respectful in his private life. He does not say too much or make many comments.

"Regarding public benefit, he is dutiful to whatever should be discussed. He does not lord over his subordinates or flatter his superiors. He always presents himself with proper manners and proper clothing in different circumstances."

"A spiritually developed one regularly cleans his dwelling and his body. He eats clean food and regulates his thoughts as an important spiritual practice. He is more serious about internal spiritual practice than external rituals or any religious promotion."

"A spiritually developed one does not eat unclean or spoiled food. He knows overeating is unsupportive to the body and hurts the flow of chi, which is termed as 'life energy.'"

"A spiritually developed one does not talk while eating and when lying down to sleep. This habit can be built by eating and sleeping alone."

"Before a spiritually developed one takes his meal, he keeps quiet, sitting for a few minutes in order to offer the food to the spiritual energy of his life before he consumes it. His meal may consist of simple vegetables, fruit, soup and grain, yet the spiritual practice of offering the meal makes it equal to a bountiful festival for a universal divinity. He sits upright when he eats alone or with people. He does not lose control by overeating or eating wastefully, which would supply more nutrition than his body actually needs."

"When a spiritually developed person is at home, he relaxes himself and is natural. When he is sleeping, he does not lay face up like a corpse."

"A spiritually developed one has sympathy to those who have lost a family member. His movements are gentle and kind while around the blind and disabled."

"A spiritually developed one does not engage in activities requiring great concentration during times of heavy storms, thunder, strong winds or earthquakes, except those special endeavors done out of necessity."

"When a spiritually developed one drives a car, he watches the road. When he sits in a car, he stays quiet and does not move around too much."

"If a spiritually developed one enters a place where he is not accepted, he departs quickly like a bird flying away. He goes where he is accepted. He never presents himself as a pest on any occasion."

"A spiritually developed one would rather admire the freedom of the birds than eat their sweet meat.

"He is the one who can accept a gift of love. It does not mean he loves gifts."

CHAPTER TWELVE

Attune One's Spiritual Energy

"A spiritually developed one would rather follow a simple social approach rather than a complicated, superficial social code that teaches hypocrisy."

"A spiritually developed one and his friends do not need to be recognized by society at large. They respect and value their spiritual independence."

"A spiritually developed teacher is enlightened by the questions of his students. The students of a spiritually developed teacher are enlightened by the answers from the teacher. Thus, enlightenment is realized, though the contents of the enlightenment of the student and the teacher are different."

"Good behavior comes from inside out. This is illustrated by the conduct of a student of spiritual development. He was experiencing difficulty in his own family. After his mother passed away, his father remarried. The step mother treated the boy poorly, but was very good to her own two natural sons. The boy held no resentment towards the step mother and the two step brothers. When his father discovered the reality of the mistreatment, he decided to drive out the woman and her two sons. However, the boy begged the father not to do that on account of him. The step mother and the sons were greatly moved and thus changed totally.

"It is not war among family members that makes a change. It was true sincerity and love that brought about a good ending."

"A black spot on white jade can be removed by grinding. A dark spot on one's character is hard to remove. Rather than removing one's black spots, do not create them in the first place."

"A truly developed one teaches the direct path of spiritual development to people rather than exalting a religion of spiritual government that creates dependence."

"This is the subject of a true, good and fruitful life that a spiritually developed one cares about and works for: attaining helpful knowledge and improving his life. He does not wastefully extend his imagination about the afterlife or previous lives, because he has no more doubt about this life or the life of any other time."

"When his internal energy shines from inside out, a student of spiritual development feels respectful, peaceful, happy and flowing. He does not experience stagnation."

"A spiritually developed person says and does what is reasonable and applicable to the situation at hand."

"A student of spiritual development does not stop when he reaches the door of learning and think that he has achieved enough. Nor does he stop in the hallway and feel that he has attained all that he can. In his spiritual learning, he goes through the door, down the hall and reaches into the depth of the inner-most room where he finds the most precious treasure of spiritual development."

"There are generally two ways that people express themselves in life. One is to be weak; that is not strong enough. The other is to be overly aggressive; that is overly impulsive. Both ways miss the center of a balanced life. Like arrows, few fly to the correct spot where a life of spiritual balance is lived."

"A spiritually developed one does not help the one who is in a powerful position to obtain more material wealth by using any special privileges entrusted to him."

"A spiritually developed one would be happy with his simple life earned by righteous means rather than becoming rich by unrighteous ones."

"Though a good person is agreeable to most situations of life, if he does not follow the path of spiritual development, he is only partially enlightened."

"True sincerity is the essence of spiritual development in life; it is not merely the expression on a person's face or the fancy words he shows to others."

"A spiritually developing one would rather consult with a developed person than risk making an unclear action."

"A student of spiritual development dares not give his life away unless he clearly knows the purpose of the action."

"A spiritually developed one would quit his job for righteous reasons. He will not be a disrespected tool for a person with a bad purpose."

"It does not help to give a big, important position to an immature person."

"A student of spiritual development does not take pride in being above people nor in holding a large piece of territory.   Most important to him is spiritual development."

"A spiritually developed one can defend his small country from the big countries. He can improve the starving of his nation and guide his people to freedom."

"A spiritually developed person can make it possible for people to enjoy self-sufficiency and reach the awakening of spiritual development."

"A spiritually developed person can conduct people in spiritual learning and lead them to spiritual good order."

"A spiritually developed one can enjoy playing a simple instrument with peaceful music to amuse himself and tune his own spiritual energy. He can be happy watching young people swimming in the river and visiting the forest."

"A student asked his teacher, 'Who do you respect most in the world?' The teacher replied, 'The people I respect do not need to be rich and noble, or poor to attract my sympathy. The people I respect are psychologically, spiritually and physically healthy; that is normal when you live in the world. Basically, health inside and outside is the most valuable thing; it is above being rich and noble or sagely.'"

CHAPTER THIRTEEN

Keep to Your Spiritual Nature

"A student of spiritual development knows his pursuit to be the realization of the integral truth of the universe. In order to do this, he must first attain the heart of no partiality. The heart of no partiality reaches Heaven. It depends on self-discipline and the removing of all personal obstructions and the extending of personal achievement outwardly to meet all people of the world; thus, natural harmony is fulfilled. With the embodiment of the integral truth of the universe, all life is prosperous."

"A student of spiritual development knows his goal and works to reach it. If something is not right, he does not look at it. If it does not sound right, he does not listen to it. If it is not a correct thing, he does not talk about it. If it is not right action, he does not do it. If a thing or a person is not right, he even does not think of it. This is the way he reaches Tao.

'How do you know what is right?' a student asked.

'You know what is right by your rightful being,' was the answer."

"A student of spiritual development in the world is like a visitor away from home. When he asks people to do things for him, it is like his praying: he does not demand. He does nothing to people that he does not like to do unto himself. He does not complain in his country or at home. He is not assertive in talking."

"A student of spiritual development does not need to worry or frown. Because of his self-inspection, there is no wrongdoing in his life. Thus, he has no vexation or fear."

"A student of spiritual development does not fear the social isolation caused by disassociating from a friend or brother who does wrong to people or the world."

"Do not be concerned about the length of your life; it is decided by your personal nature. Do not be concerned about becoming rich and empowered; it is decided by how much support you can have from your environment. It is important to have your personal interests and extend an effort in a healthy and suitable direction to make your life enjoyable."

"A spiritually developed person respects whatever he can reach. He respects people and is kind with the world. In any situation, he offers help indiscriminately. Thus, a spiritually developed one does not feel troubled if there is no one to make him his teacher."

"A spiritually developed one does not let his clarity of mind become disturbed, even when false information is continually given to him. He remains impervious to the bad and the false and restores his clarity each time he receives such influence. Like the vast blue sky, he may sometimes be clouded heavily with dark clouds. However, after the summer shower, he regains his clarity immediately. He does not let his independent and unobstructed vision be destroyed by a cloud from inside or outside."

"A good government is a government trusted by its people. It leads its country to a self-sufficient respectable life for all and maintains efficient defense of the nation. This is made possible by sponsoring a healthy and complete education of its people which provides the opportunities of physical, intellectual and spiritual development.

"In case a government cannot afford to do all of these, it can consider reducing military strength. In cases where a government cannot maintain a good material condition for all its people, the education and spiritual development of the society is the first priority and must be supported. With suitable education and spiritual development, a nation always reaches its appropriate place."

"A government or an individual who has attained great physical strength is like a tiger: the king of most other animals. Even though he has displays power in his mighty appearance, unless he also attains spiritual development, he is like a paper tiger with no bones or blood. He lacks the real foundation of a complete life being."

"An intellectually developed person is like a piece of lion's fur cut off from the hide.

"The hide and the fur are not separable; if they were, they would not be valued. Just as the hide and fur should not be separated, complete development must include personal physical health, and intellectual and spiritual well being."

"The tongue of an irresponsible politician is faster than the top speed of a fast horse. His behavior lags far behind his tongue. When a task demands righteousness and courage, his actions are slow like the movement of a 3,000 year old turtle.

"A spiritually developed one would rather see something realized than just talk about it."

"A king was having a discussion with a spiritually developed one and asked, 'What should I do when my government does not have enough money to do all the important things?'

"The developed one replied, 'Use the ancient, time-honored tax method of taking a tenth from the people's production,' was the answer.

"'Taking two-tenths is still not enough, not to mention one,' said the king.

"'Decrease the tax, attract people to till the land and invest in your country. This means: increase the revenue by decreasing it. When all people have enough, the government has enough. When people do not have enough, how can the government have enough? Too much tax is self-robbery in that it does not nurture the strength of people to pay the tax."

"In choosing the proper way to do something, one should not allow emotion or preference to make the decision. It is necessary to be open to all useful knowledge; inspect it carefully and do not be confused by general information."

"Good administration of a country requires the proper fulfillment of duty to avoid trouble. Otherwise, the normalcy and health of the administration and the nation will be lost. The government of a country is what determines whether or not there is peace, order and normalcy in society."

"A person who has no unfulfilled promise seldom finds any argument in his life."

"Everybody in an argument is the same: each one looks to win. The true winner, however, is the one who does not argue."

"A good administration can be achieved by the one who is serious and untiring in work and who has the highest loyalty."

"A spiritually developed one is the one who gives help in accomplishing only positive and beneficial things. The spiritually undeveloped do the opposite."

"An effective and respectable administration wishes to do right and be upright; then there will be no wrongdoing. If there is, usually the mistakes are correctable."

"A king of a small country was annoyed by the many thieves in his land. He consulted with a spiritually developed one asking what to do about them.   The solution was, 'Lessen your interest in obtaining more goods, but help the people of your country to obtain more.   Then there will be no thieves.'"

"A serviceable government does not kill people; an evil one does. A serviceable government holds as its goal to serve the people; the evil one makes people serve its power and imposes its ideology on them."

"The influence of good leadership is like a breeze that gently blows on the grass. The grass is not damaged. Bad government is like a flood; it washes the life of the vegetation away."

"A student asked a developed one how a person can be prosperous. 'What do you mean by prosperity?' he asked the student. The student replied, 'To be respected in your town.'

"To be renowned in one's town or country is reputation, not prosperity,' commented the developed one. 'The prosperity of a spiritually developed person lies in keeping his spiritual nature. He supports whatever is righteous. He is considerate. He does not compete with evil means. He is often a person who is prosperous in his family and society.

"To be reputed is different than prosperity. Adopting the popular faith without looking into its truthfulness, a person of reputation may look very religious and kind because he supports the undeveloped conventions without a true sense of duty. He may become well liked among people in the society.'"

"To be kind is to love people. To be wise is to understand oneself."

"A young man went to a spiritually developed one and asked how to make a respectful profit, how to discipline himself and how to keep from running into trouble. The answer was, 'A respectful profit is the reward of honest, good, hard work. Disciplining oneself is to start to remove all one's bad habits. Keeping out of trouble is not allowing one's anger to ignite the fire of a fight."

"Bad leadership is established by bad people to control good people. Good leadership lets the good people serve all people. To put good people in public positions encourages people to do good.

"Putting bad people in high positions intimidates others from doing right. In the end, their influence will degenerate society like allowing the landing of a pirate ship to plunder a town."

"A good leader looks for good people. The good people also look for him.

"A bad leader looks for bad people. The bad people also look for him.

"A good leader succeeds by being good and engaging in good leadership. A bad leader succeeds by being bad and engaging in bad leadership.

"However, the good leader enjoys a healthy society as the fruit of his labors. The bad leader finally tastes bad fruit."

"If good advice is given but not heeded, no further advice is given."

"A developed person makes friends for shared intellectual or spiritual interests. Only spiritually developed people can assist each other deeply as friends. Spiritually undeveloped and underdeveloped people also make friends; but very soon, they become enemies over profit conflicts or personality conflicts."

CHAPTER FOURTEEN

Good Leadership is Nature

"A student asked a spiritually developed one, 'How do you recognize good leadership qualities in a person?' He replied, 'A good leader is the first person to work at resolving a problem. He makes no excuses; he works hard. He never tires of dedicating his life to the benefit of others.'"

"The same question was presented to another spiritually developed one. He replied, 'You can recognize a good leader by his good attitude towards working, which provides a good example for others. He forgives the small mistakes of his subordinates and gives authority to those of responsibility and capability.'

"The student asked, 'How can you know who are the people of responsibility and capability?' He answered, 'Pick those whom you already know are responsible and capable. Then no one will like to stay away from you, because you are so knowledgeable and appreciating.'"

"When the king was away attending to difficulties at the border of his kingdom, the prince took the opportunity to seize the throne. He then asked a spiritually developed one for help in setting up a new administration to replace his father's. The developed one replied, 'Such a thing cannot be done. One who takes power by stealing cannot expect honesty from his subordinates. One who damages his own father cannot expect the respect of his children. One who uses violence cannot expect a long period of peace. It takes correct motivation and correct means to establish a good administration. Because this situation lacks the good qualities needed for government, I cannot be of help to you.'

"The prince said, 'However, my father took his throne from his father the same way.' The developed one said, 'How would it be if your son takes the throne from you in the same way? Would it please you that I serve him, also?'"

"In the ancient natural world, when the principle means of living changed from herding to agriculture, new communities were formed based on the learning experience of agricultural life. Thus, small kingdoms were begun. An ambitious young man wished to use similar ways to gather people and become a leader of such a community. He expressed his desire to a spiritually developed one. The developed one said, 'Teaching cooperative agricultural life on the free land is not the only condition for forming a new community. There is one more fundamental requirement. It is to develop and extend a positive personality. That is what will attract a following of people. By being polite, people will respect you. By being righteous, people will not go against you. By being faithful, people will not abandon you. The combination of all of these will inspire people from the four directions to bring their children to join you.'"

"In leading a natural community, the enjoyment of folk songs and simple music can produce the joy of natural life. Uplifting folk songs and music are the true religion of people. They help people more than rigid religious and political influence, which only attempt to manage or control people. When people are in harmony, why would anyone compete to be the head of the society as a political leader? When everybody is experiencing enjoyment, the leader is the one who is on the lookout for the kinds of problems that may occur on such occasions."

"Political leadership, if it is upright, does not have an ideology too elevated or too far removed from natural reality. However, if those in authority are the wrong people for the job, what ideology can actually work to improve the life condition of a society?"

"A spiritually developed person attunes himself to live as simply as suitable in his personal or home life. He does not expect everything to be perfect for him. When he has enough to live on, his self-contentment helps him attune his emotions and ambitions to the reality of life. Thus, he acquires the concentration for spiritual cultivation."

"A country can be developed by taking advantage of its material resources, but its people and their development is its most important resource. People of a country can be developed through education, both intellectual and spiritual. By educating its people, a country will be truly developed."

"A society that can stop using capital punishment is a society that provides a complete education, both intellectual and spiritual."

"When spiritual development has been reached by the majority of people, a truly peaceful world will be realized."

"The highest welfare of a natural free society is achieved through bringing peace and order into the lives of all people. However, evil competition of political leadership damages the harmony among people. If this highest goal cannot be realized for the people, leadership brings no true value to the world."

"'Is there any one thing that can make my nation become prosperous?' A king asked a spiritually developed one. He replied, 'I do not know of such a good thing. But if a king or a person in authority knew to keep the prosperity of the nation in his mind and was careful to attain this goal, the nation will find prosperity along the way."

"'Is there any one word that can cause one to lose his kingdom?' The king asked the spiritually developed one.

"He replied, 'I do not think there is such powerful word, but close to it is 'I do what I like. No one can disobey my order.' That is enough to destroy a kingdom.

"'A king is not always wise. He can be right or wrong. Why not allow people to point out his mistakes?'"

"'What is the art of politics?' asked a student of a spiritually developed one.

"He replied, 'Politics is the support you gather from the people who live near you. They are unhappy living on the foundation laid for them before by somebody else. If you can truly help, you not only earn their support, but people who live in other places will also want to move close to you and give you support.'"

"How can I achieve myself?' asked the student.

"The developed one replied, 'Do not be speedy. Do not focus on small losses. One cannot move fast when being hasty. You cannot take the larger gain when you pay too much attention to the small profits and the small losses.'"

"'I am proud to see the righteous in my region. When a father stole a sheep, his son bore witness to the crime,' said a governor to a spiritually developed one.

"'What I am happy to see in the righteousness of the people is that when the father steals the sheep, the son is willing to receive the punishment for his father's mistake, but the father will not let him do it,' was the reply of the developed one."

"A spiritually developed one respects the person who maintains self-discipline, is always respectful and is loyal. He might be from a different spiritual custom or come from a foreign land, but I do not look upon him with prejudice or cut off friendly association with him for that reason."

"'How can I recognize a person of spiritual development?' asked a young man of his teacher.

"'A student of spiritual development knows what should and should not be done. He accomplishes his goal without degrading his character. He is harmonious and friendly with all. He keeps his word and is decisive in action. He is not a person who chases small or short-term profit.'"

"Spiritual development can be attained by a person of balance. Spiritual development can be taught to a student who is ambitious to learn and make progress. Such a person is prudent in behavior."

"A person who lacks persistence and perseverance cannot be a good student of spiritual development. Without constancy in one's learning, one cannot overcome the difficult and reach attainment. Without consistency in one's work, one cannot make improvements. And without constancy in one's character, one will fall when exposed to temptation."

"Spiritually developed ones are harmonious with different kinds of people and accept their differences. Spiritually undeveloped people befriend only people exactly like them, so they do not learn to achieve harmony."

"A spiritually developed person does not necessarily win the approval or agreement of all the people in the world. Nor is he necessarily disapproved of by all the people in the world. He is the one approved of by all the good people and disapproved of by all the bad people."

"It is not hard or bad to work for a spiritually achieved boss, because he understands what you can do. He knows you better than you do yourself. He is not pleased, however, if you choose improper means to accomplish the work and to attain the goal."

"It is difficult and not difficult to work for a boss of low character because he asks more than you can accomplish. However, he is easily pleased by whatever means, even low ones, you choose in accomplishing the work and attaining his goal."

"A spiritually developed one might look hard to approach but he will not become a problem in your life. The spiritually inferior one might be easy to approach, but he will become a problem for you someday."

"A spiritually developed one is upright, persistent and straight. His good qualities might make people feel uncomfortable; however, he is loving."

"The students of spiritual development help one another with serious discussion and by correcting each other. They love each another more than natural brothers."

"A spiritually developed teacher guides people to be productive, to work at any constructive livelihood, and to defend their safety. He teaches them to attain spiritual development but not to become a dependent. Dependence is viewed by him as self-abandonment."

CHAPTER FIFTEEN

Spiritual Insufficiency is a Disgrace

"A student asked his teacher, 'When does a spiritually developed one feel disgraced?' The teacher replied, 'He feels disgraced when he works and receives a salary from a government that practices an extreme ideology and that pushes people in an extreme direction.'"

"A person of aggressive personality, self-pride, extensive personal desire and who easily makes enemies over small things is not one of spiritual development. Such a one must overcome the restrictions of an unrefined and inconsiderate personality."

"To attain spiritual development, it is most important to become harmless to other people. It is also important to become helpful to others.

"This is the disgrace of a spiritual developed person: In a moral society and an appropriate situation, one cannot offer all one's energy for the improvement of the human world. In a harmful society and an adverse situation, one cannot disassociate from the tyrannical ruling system.

"In the latter circumstance, one should withdraw to nurture one's character, but not take the support of or join the tyrannical ruling class."

"A spiritually developed one is not overly attentive to the comforts of his own life. When he lives in a good society, he can fully extend his righteous influence in all circumstances. In a bad society, he remains righteous in his own life activities. Although society has became confused, he does not change his virtuous ways or exploit a situation for personal advantage."

"A spiritually developed one dares to speak out for righteousness. But not all those who dare to speak out are truly for righteousness.

"A spiritually developed one is brave concerning what should be done. He is not hesitant to give his life-energy to accomplish what is right. He does not impair his righteous soul by being attached to his body's life. Though there are many brave people, not all brave people are righteous."

"Powerful conquerors of the world find that their expansion ends quickly. Those who work to guide people towards a good healthy life leave a lasting influence."

"In the process of spiritual development, a person sometimes makes a mistake by being disoriented in a specific situation. However, he immediately finds a way to restore himself from the momentary confusion. A person who remains confined to the narrow interest of personal profit hardly benefits or learns from his own lifetime."

"When a spiritually developed one loves a young person he makes that person work diligently and effectively to bring out his virtuous qualities. When a spiritually developed one has loyalty for someone, he is not afraid to give advice to correct the person's errors even if it might hurt the feelings of that person."

"It is easy for a rich person to forget the troubles he has been through. It is good for him to remember his past and have sympathy for those still struggling.
"It is a steep road for a person in an impover- ished condition, either materially or spiritually. He must gather his own strength to make improvement in his life. Sooner or later, he must be the one who works out his own problems."

"To develop wholeness and perfection, one must be knowledgeable, self-contented instead of greedy, brave instead of cowardly, develop a high enjoyment for arts, music and dance, and be self-disciplined."

"In a confusing world, a virtuous person is the one when he sees profit also sees whether it is ob- tained righteously. When he sees danger, the virtu- ous person still takes an assignment that will benefit many without considering personal security. He knows what is going to be suitably fulfilled."

"A virtuous person talks at the right time, so nobody is tired of his talking. He laughs at the ap- propriate moment, so no one is tired of his laughing. He takes only what is rightfully his, so nobody dis- likes what he is doing."

"A faithful person who is righteous is not hypocritical."

"A spiritually developed one is not easily understood and he does not talk about sacrificing his life for people."

"A spiritually developed person in public service will recommend that a talented subordinate receive a position equal to his own."

"If an unrighteous ruler seizes power, yet places effective, worthy people in his administration, his rule has a chance to survive for a time."

"A person who keeps bragging without shame is not a person who can accomplish anything for other people."

"A government should not cheat the people. A government should not conflict with the wishes of its own people."

"The difference between those of spiritual development and undevelopment is that the former move upward and the latter move downward.

"The upward moving ones reach righteousness and benefit. They see the root and the trunk of life, which guides them toward attaining spiritual development.

"The downward moving ones see the branches and twigs of life. They miss the main achievement and work for small profit."

"Spiritual development assists one's own life. Worldly learning is what sounds and looks good to other people."

"A spiritually developed one is not afraid of being imperfect, but he tries to minimize his mistakes; though he be perfectly virtuous, he never expects to be exalted as a perfect model. People have no need or demand to become perfect according to an external standard. However, it is only natural to return to our own innate perfection."

"A dutiful person attends to his own responsibility before extending help to others. He does not interfere in the duties of others."

"A spiritually developed one feels shame if his words exceed his conduct."

"Spiritual development manifests in: being natural hearted in order not to worry, being wise in order not to be perplexed and being brave in order not to be afraid. If he has not attained these three, a person lives with worry, perplexity or fear. When he has achieved all three, a person truly reaches the integral virtue of spiritual nature."

"A student of spiritual development works on his spiritual progress. He does not waste time and energy talking about other people's evil or problems."

"A student of spiritual development is not concerned if other people do not know about his progress. He is concerned if he is unable to make progress."

"A person cannot prevent another person from cheating. But he can prevent being cheated by his own overextended desire for profit or being seduced by time and labor-saving conveniences or by wishful thinking.

"Also, a person cannot guess whether another person can be trusted. He himself must make sure whether or not there will be some unforeseen changes that could happen in relation to that person he wishes to trust. The changes he must look for are things that would render the person unable to meet his obligations.

"The attainment of security in a relationship with another cannot rely totally on one's own experience of that person; it is dependant upon one's developing foreknowledge and objectivity regarding changes."

"If a spiritually developed one is busy on a world-wide trip, it is not to further his personal gain; it is his constant effort to improve the unhealthy situation of the world."

"A good horse is powerful, swift and, above all, cooperative."

"It is the highest virtue to return goodness and kindness to an evil doer. Yet it is also proper to treat an evil doer with straightness. It is correct to return good and kind behavior to those who have been kind and favorable to you."

"A spiritually developed person is not frustrated if only a few people can understand or appreciate him. In a time of darkness, he can live a quiet life and make no complaint. He does not expect a high position from worldly, powerful leaders. He always returns to the basics in order to keep moving upward in his spiritual development. In this way, he reaches the essence of all life."

"A wise one does not serve tyranny or participate in an improper government. He leaves if his advice is not respected or accepted. He moves away when he is not correctly understood and judged."

"There is another kind of wise man who knows that even if a situation in human society cannot be helped immediately, there is still a need for him to do what would be helpful in the long term."

"In a bad time, the wise one does not feel ashamed to live with an ordinary job. He would not take a high position and join in the corrupt ruling class."

"Once a teacher of development amused himself playing music on a group of earthen jars. He tapped different size jars to produce different tones, and tapped different parts on a single jar to produce different resonances.

"A peddler of housewares, practically an achieved one, passed his door and heard the sounds. He commented: "He is amusing himself, but the music expresses his frustration as a teacher.' Then, he continued, 'The player has the high ambition that the world will listen to his teaching and advice. But if the world does not value what he says, why should he be bothered? In such a situation, is it not better just to take care of your own life?

"'The ancient ballad says, "When the water is deep, you wade. Even with rolled up clothes, you may still get wet and maybe drown. When the water is shallow, you wade with rolled up clothes and go safely across. So if the time is right, you can go ahead to make the crossing. When the time is not right, it is better not to do it unless you are prepared to drown and be washed away."'

"One student of this teacher heard the comments and reported them to his teacher. The teacher said, 'It is true. If I follow his advice and do not keep thinking about the troubles of the world, I will have no frustration.'

"However, the teacher did not give up his purpose, despite his temporary frustrations."

"When a government is doing right and sets everything right for itself, the people easily bring order into their own lives."

"A spiritually developed person is the one who disciplines himself seriously. Higher achievement comes to one who disciplines himself in order to help those in his surroundings enjoy peace and love. The highest achievement is the one who disciplines himself to help all others in the world have a good life."

CHAPTER SIXTEEN

Learning to Know
is not Spiritual Development

"It is helpful for a spiritual student to learn some essential spiritual practices and rituals in accordance with the high principles of Taoist strategy as expressed by Lao Tzu, Sun Tzu, etc., to deploy and channel his spiritual energy, to guide group activities and for martial art training. These can help the student toward achieving spiritual fulfillment in worldly life."

"Even spiritually developed people meet difficulties and bad situations. They respond by holding firm to their principles. They are not like the undeveloped ones who merely help themselves expediently in a situation."

"The impression that most people have of a developed one is that he knows everything. In reality, knowing everything is not a sign of spiritual development. Rather, spiritual development is a universal understanding that is deeper than intellectual knowledge. It is a kind of integration, an achievement quite the opposite of being scattered or fragmented by mere book learning. It exists above superficial discussion or exploration.

"Some people who are very knowledgeable have only attained intellectual development and have not experienced spiritual integralness. Only the spiritually developed one has escaped from behind the conceptual walls which keep one from experiencing the integral truth."

"When spiritual integration is applied to the world's problems, it produces the best possible solutions, above those of worldly leaders. True solutions can only be found through right understanding by all moral worldly leaders of human society and by not being partial or playing favorites. True benefit occurs when beneficial and applicable ways of solving problems have been found and applied to society. This is called being governed by the principle of wu wei or naturalness. It is to do nothing extra."

"When spiritual integration is applied in personal behavior, one becomes aware that good or correct behavior comes from one's own development. His conduct comes to accord with what he says. A person of spiritual integration will be trusted in a foreign place just as he is trusted by the people of his home town."

"The way of a spiritually developed one is as direct as an arrow flying out towards its target. However, a spiritually developed one offers his talents to his society only when the right leadership invites him. At other times, he withdraws himself, his talent and capability, and keeps it like a scroll book that can be rolled up and kept tightly hidden in one's bosom. During that time, he has no communication with tyranny."

"Give advice to the right person when it is correct; otherwise you will miss the opportunity to help.

"In some situations, no advice should be given. If it is given, it is wrong for both you and the recipient.

"A spiritually developed one is watchful in all types of situations regarding giving advice."

"A spiritually developed person does not damage his spiritual virtue by pursuing physical pleasure or to benefit his bodily life. He would rather fulfill his spiritual virtue by giving up his physical pleasure or giving up his physical life."

"Realizing one's spiritual purpose in the world is like being a good craftsman who becomes accomplished after first choosing the right tools. In realizing one's spiritual or virtuous goal in a society, a person needs the help of all good people and also needs to gather the friendly energy of the wise."

"In realizing a spiritual life, absorb any helpful achievements and good teachings that are available to assist the different aspects of your life. Do away with harmful, bad habits and lower interests; adopt good music to replace the bad. The developed one knows that good music is healing and bad music can make you sick."

"A spiritually developed one disciplines himself with strictness and complains little about others."

"When a student of spiritual development meets a problem, he keeps looking for the best solution."

"A person who acts impulsively does not give careful consideration to the result of his actions. He enjoys being with people that do not discuss anything truly helpful. He likes his cleverness to be recognized, though he always brings it to bear on unimportant, minor things rather than offering real benefit to others. That is not the way to reach spiritual development."

"The student of spiritual development is a person of upright life, correct behavior, humble output and faithful accomplishment. In attaining those, he is achieved spiritually."

"The student of spiritual development knows it is foolish if he wastes his life without accomplishing anything that is serviceable to others."

"When there is difficulty between two parties, the spiritually developed one looks to correct his own part of the trouble. The undeveloped one concentrates on the other person's fault."

"A student of spiritual development respects himself. He does not engage in struggling with people. He is happy with all people. He does not join a group for the purpose of contention."

"If there is one word to be followed by the student of spiritual development, it is to forgive. If there is one principle to be followed by the student of spiritual development, it is not to do to others what you yourself dislike."

"A spiritually developed one does not comment about any other person casually. He does not judge well or ill of a person unless he has had experience with the person. Yet he knows that his experience of that person is still partial.

"He is fair to all. That is the straight way of all ancient spiritually developed ones."

"Also, a spiritually developed one does not easily commit himself to another person. He does not judge another unless he has experience of that person, and even then, he knows that his experience is only partial.

"The straight way of the spiritually developed one is to be fair to all."

"In listening to an argument, some things will be missed and even unclear. You cannot make a new solution for an old problem unless you bring about a new understanding.

"In your personal life, opportunities will be missed and mistakes made. The horse that ran away many years ago should be forgotten, because the new moment at hand is the most precious life that you are living. It is foolish to use new life to argue old disputes. New friendship is much more important than old problems and the past."

"A flowery tongue destroys an honest character."

"The one who cannot tolerate small problems cannot accomplish a great task."

"Even if a person is accepted by all the people, a spiritually developed one still needs to observe the person himself. A thing or a person is known by the sum of its actions. A spiritually developed person looks into each matter or person himself; he does not follow what other people say. He relies on his independent judgement."

"It is truth that enlightens people. It is wisdom to make the truth understood to other people."

"If the trouble of a person is not corrected, it is truly trouble."

"A student of spiritual development does not sit alone thinking and fasting all day and all night in order to become wise. Good thought can only be produced while also doing and learning in the world."

"A spiritually developed one puts himself to work in a good life direction without thinking of the reward. He sets his mind and thought to find a good way to accomplish work for the benefit of others, not for his own material wealth."

"The student of spiritual development enjoys his work. His reward is produced naturally from his work and his concentration in learning; that is the achievement. This achievement comes through serious learning, although sometimes no external success is seen. He mainly enjoys the good work and the good learning which in itself is rewarding and satisfying to him."

"A king may be clever enough to attain his throne. If his character is not good enough, he will lose it soon after by gathering only poisons and evils.

"If a king is clever and has a good character, but he does not love the people, he will not be supported.

"Although all three requirements are there - being clever, having a good character and loving people - unless there is a good system for administration, the kingdom will still fall."

"A student of spiritual development may not be clever enough to do anything for himself, but he can be entrusted with an important responsibility. An undeveloped one may be clever enough, but cannot be entrusted with the responsibility for accomplishing an important task.

"Cleverness serves oneself. Spiritual development serves all."

"The importance of spiritual development can be compared to the importance of water and fire in people's daily life. Water and fire are basic to life, but if they are not carefully managed, trouble might occur. However, it has never been the case that spiritual development has caused harm. Thus, spiritual development in people's life is more important than water and fire."

"In regard to spiritual duty, a student does not yield to his teacher."

"A spiritually developed one may be not understood, but he will not change his principle of righteousness."

"In serving the public, keep your focus on working well rather than on hunting for profit."

"In education, there should be not any discrimination."

"If their spiritual goals are different, people cannot remain or work together very long."

"In giving a speech, be expressive and communicable, but do not employ cunning."

CHAPTER SEVENTEEN

People Create Opportunity

"Opportunity has never been equal for everyone. A developing one creates opportunity. A false hero is created by an opportunity."

"The wise one does not let opportunity crown him. When it is lost, he does not let it strip off his robe. This is why he is selective about the opportunities he accepts."

"The cunning one uses opportunity, but he is also used by the opportunity."

"It is a mistake for a student of spiritual development to assist the aggression of his nation toward a peaceful neighboring country.

"It is the duty of people with spiritual development not to support the use of military strength; such would be like releasing a fierce tiger into a city crowd. Damage to good life is inevitable. This would be the spiritual responsibility of the aggressive nation.

"When an improper decision is made by a leader, it is everyone's duty not to wait and see a stumbling society fall into danger."

"The prosperity of a society is not its problem: its problem is that too many people have no opportunity to improve their lives.

"It is not a problem for most people to live a simple life. The problem is to have a peaceful environment that is supportive enough to provide opportunities that allow people to improve. When equality of opportunity is reached, no one will be left out. When harmony is reached, there will be no contention among people. When spiritual development of people is reached, there will be no danger in life. This is the great human society.

"When a society is developed like this, it is its duty to help the other countries through a friendly, spiritual approach. Let all people of the entire world share peace and prosperity."

"There are three character traits that a friend can have. A beneficial friend is honest, understanding or knowledgeable, and wise. A harmful one is hypocritical, dishonest, or talks without true knowledge."

"Three kinds of pleasures are beneficial to a person. They are the pleasures of self-discipline, of seeing and talking in the positive mode of life and having good friends. There are also three harmful pleasures. They are the pleasures of self-pride in speaking ill of other people, idleness and obsessive eating and drinking."

"A student of spiritual development may have three problems. The first is impatience, which is speaking about something before having attained or comprehended it. The second is holding back in making progress or not speaking about something

when it could cause trouble later. This is the attitude of self-evasion or denial. The third is insensi-
tivity, talking to people but not being aware of the
corresponding response."

"There are three warnings to a student of spiritual development. In his youth, before maturing
physically and psychologically, he must be careful
not to indulge in sexual fantasy. When he is an
adult and he feels strong, he must not impulsively
engage in meaningless physical adventures or fighting. When he is old and his vigor is weaker, he
should avoid greed and extending himself for material gain and possessions."

"A student of spiritual development has three
great fears. He fears not fulfilling his duty in developing himself, not learning from a good example and
not following the wisdom of spiritual achievement.
"Young people who do not keep themselves growing in a healthy direction will grow unhealthily.
They do not know that the way of a positive, constructive life is to tend to one's duty. If they disre-
spect the good examples, they do not value the wisdom of spiritual achievement."

"One who is wise naturally and spiritually is
highly evolved. One who is wise by learning is still
elevated. One who meets trouble and attains wisdom from the experience is respectable. But if the
one who meets trouble still does not respect wisdom
and does not work on his personal improvement, he
is hopeless."

"There are eight guidelines for a student of spiritual development. When he sees a thing, he sees clearly. When he hears a thing, he hears clearly. When he greets people, he is respectful. When he speaks to people, he is sincere. When he does a thing, he concentrates. When he has doubt, he makes the matter clear. When he is angry, he controls himself even if this is difficult. When an opportunity arises for his personal gain, he thinks of righteousness."

"There are few people who are eager to improve themselves and avoid evil like scalding water. There are few people who do not join the contention for worldly profit and who prefer to live peacefully and quietly working on their spiritual development and supporting other people."

"There were people who owned thousands of horses who were not remembered after they died. There are people who are always remembered because they extended their righteousness natures to others in their lives."

"People may wonder if a spiritually developed teacher teaches his own sons special things that are not offered to other students. The truth is that he teaches his sons spiritual development in the same way as he teaches all other students."

"The purity of human nature is equal in importance to the natural environment. It is the environment that people are born into and grow up in that makes them very different.

"Most people adapt to changes either well or poorly without making any spiritual effort. Yet wise ones do not let the negative elements in an environment change them.

"Foolish and stubborn people do not let the positive elements in the teachings of the wise help them. This is an important difference among people."

"A student of spiritual development should add these finer virtues into his natural character: self-respect, tolerance, faithfulness, effectiveness and being of benefit to all. Upon attaining these five good qualities, he should promote them among his friends."

"There are six obstacles a student of spiritual development should break through: 1) Being fond of kindness but not learning the proper way of fulfillment; the obstacle is stupidity. 2) Being fond of knowledge without the power of discrimination; the obstacle is scatteredness. 3) Being fond of faithfulness without clearly examining the nature of the person or matter he has faith in; the obstacle is harmful prejudice. 4) Being fond of directness without the vision of a correct outcome; the obstacle is impulsiveness. 5) Being fond of bravery without the knowledge of self-control; the obstacle is violence. 6) Being fond of strength without interfering in other people's lives; the obstacle is craziness."

"It is helpful for young people to learn healthy songs and poems and any positive art that will expand the reaches of their individual emotions, provide healthy growth and bring them close to other people."

"A person who appears very upright superficially, but is internally greedy for the possessions of other people, is a person of inferior spiritual character. Sometimes such a person can make a whole community believe he is good. He is, however, a thief of nature."

"To pick up rumors and pass them along without examining them is to abandon one's personal truthful nature."

"A person of spiritual inferiority holding public office is not motivated by care about real benefit for his people and his country. He is only concerned about obtaining personal benefit from the position."

"A student of spiritual development may have three problems. He may be self-proud and forget small details such as responding to people's thanks. He may be too serious and make other people feel uncomfortable. He may be naive and thus be too direct and offensive in what he says and does.

"A person of spiritual underdevelopment may also have these three problems, but more intensified. He is self-proud to the point of neglecting important principles of his life. To him, the principles of ethics seem valueless. His seriousness becomes criticism of everything and everyone in the world. He is naive; he expects people to enjoy the tricks he plays on them."

"'Is learning to become very brave and strong regarded as a spiritual virtue?' a student asked his teacher. The teacher answered, 'Virtuous performance is decided by righteousness. A person of ambition who is brave but not righteous could create a large disturbance in the world such as the starting of an wrongful rebellion. A profit-hungry person who is brave but not righteous could become a bandit.'"

"'Does a person of spiritual development have anything that he does not agree with and so rejects?' a student asked.

"'Yes, he does,' answered his teacher. 'They are these: talking about the wrongdoing of others, scandal-mongering about someone he does not even know, using force to obtain something and being indecisive in doing what is right.'

"'What should be rejected by a student of spiritual development?' a student asked the teacher.

"'Taking another's achievement and presenting it as a product of his own intelligence; not being humble, but thinking he is straight; unnecessarily disclosing another's evil and thinking of himself as honest."

"It is hard to be with people before they have attained spiritual development.   If the wise one stays too close to them, they do not take his advice or teaching seriously; if he keeps them too far away, they will never become educated by the wise."

CHAPTER EIGHTEEN

Have Sympathy for the Unachieved

"A person who does not know to hold fast to the subtle reality of the truthful nature of life and who does not devote his life to spiritual development cannot accomplish anything meaningful. He fritters away or scatters his useful life energy."

"A student learned from a teacher that in making friends, one should accept the agreeable ones and keep away from the disagreeable ones.

"Later, the student learned from a senior student who had learned from his teacher: one should praise those who do well and have sympathy for the unachieved. It is especially important to cultivate oneself to be acceptable and agreeable. That means to increase one's tolerance to accept and agree with other people."

"It is fine for young people to do sports or play cards or chess, etc., and to be good at any of them. However, those games are not as important as working on spiritual development as the main goal of life, although those things may furnish fun and support."

"Keep learning from what is new to you. Keep reviewing what you have achieved as a result of correct timing. This is a good way of refreshing one's mind."

"Personal development can be attained through expanding one's learning and observation. The way to actualize a life of total development is to transform one's external learning and observation into objectivity rather than let it be a disturbance. One can use this objectivity in examining one's doubts and pursuing one's spiritual goals."

"All craftsmanship is accomplished by actually engaging in the work. Spiritual development is only beneficial when it is realized in daily life."

"The worst mistake of an undeveloped person is attempting to cover up and protect his mistake by lying."

"A person of spiritual development looks firm, but when he is approached, he is understanding. When he talks business, he is straight and effective."

"Spiritual development helps a leader know that first he must have the trust of people. Then he can lead people to work in the direction he guides them.

"Spiritual development helps a person to know that first he must have the trust of someone before he gives him advice. Otherwise, the other person might think the advice-giving is an attack upon him.

"The leader of spiritual undevelopment abuses people by force through not having their trust."

"With spiritual development, a person learns to hold tight to important principles of personal behavior and to be flexible in the minor details which are unimportant and less influential."

"Students of spiritual development should learn to do small chores and small errands well, and use correct manners in approaching and responding to people. If sincerity in small things is seen, the honest foundation of a personality will allow full expansion to the height of spiritual development."

"When one does well in material life it is time to reach for spiritual development. Where spiritual development is attained, one's worldly life should improve also."

"A very formal and stately looking person may not have attained spiritual development. Also, a person of spiritual development can look informal and unimpressive."

"If a person has a bad reputation, many unpleasant things may be thought to be associated with him. If a person has a good reputation, many good things may be thought to be associated with him. It is a human psychological tendency to assume that it is the good that does the good. In arriving at your conclusions, however, it is valuable to remain objective and independent."

"If a mistake is made by a developed person, he openly admits it, as the eclipse of the sun and moon is capable of being seen by all the people. When the correction of the mistake of the developed person is made, it is like the rejoining of the light of the sun and moon. This is also noticed by people."

"A spiritually developed person makes teachers out of people who have different talents and achievements."

"A student of spiritual development is careful about making a statement, because what he says might express that his knowledge about a matter is not yet complete."

"The progress of spiritual development is like someone at the fence who sees the gate. Then a few steps further, there is someone at the gate who sees the hall. Then, a few steps further, there is someone at the hall who sees the outer room. The one who has not reached the inner room cannot tell what is in it.

"So in the learning of spiritual development, there are many who see the fence and gate; they stop there and declare that they have seen everything. Thus they never make any more progress. There are few who see the hall and outer room. There are fewer still who go as far as to see the inner room.

"Therefore, spiritual development is like taking a journey into a house. Some who are at the fence see the gate. Some who are at the gate, see the hall. Some who are at the hall see the outer room. The one who has not been in the inner room never sees what is in it. Many who learn spiritual development are at the fence and gate. Few see the hall. Fewer see the inner room, but all of them think that what they have achieved is the highest."

"A spiritually developed teacher said, "In learning the integral truth, there is no fence, no door, no hall, no outer or inner room, and no partition of anything. Truthfully, there is no boundary. Yet, a searching mind can only take in a little bit at a time."

"The sky cannot be reached by using ladders, but spiritual development can be attained by different stages."

"If a spiritually developed person is in a position of leadership, he will establish good policies for the people. If he is in an ordinary job, he is dutiful and accomplishes it well. When he is alive, he is respected and loved. When he passes away, he will be remembered as a constructive model."

"The reaching of high spiritual development is like climbing a high mountain. Other kinds of achievement are like walking over a small hill. Yet, the highest spiritual development is like being in the sun, which cannot be reached by walking or climbing; people just enjoy its warmth and light."

CHAPTER NINETEEN

Keep Your Sun Shining

"The potency of life in nature is the sun. The sun in human life is the mind. If the mind is full of energy, with the healthy support of a good body, there is life. If the mind has no energy, even though a body is present, there is death. Thus, life is energy and to live is energy."

"It is necessary to have a goal in order to accomplish something. If the goal is unclear, there will be confusion. Accomplishment results from the convergence of mind with physical or material strength. The single projection of either mind or strength cannot accomplish anything."

"Love and hatred, desire and anger are four things that can cause a crisis. Thus, the wise are very prudent in using and dealing with them."

"The mind in the body is like a king. All the organs perform their different duties. The mind functions best when it remains inactive and peaceful and it is not separated from any of the dynamic subfunctions of the different organs.

"Therefore, empty yourself of desire to let the spirit enter in, eliminate the impure to let the spiritual essence stay with the mind, and live like the encompassing heaven and the receptive earth. In this way, the oneness of life and the unity of all functions is attained."

"If the bodily form is not attuned, one's spiritual potency will not be correctly poised or balanced. If quietness of mind is not maintained, the mind's unity is disturbed. When the mind is quiet, the spiritual essence stays with the bodily life. If you keep your body-house clean, the internal essence will grow and the nature spirits will come to you. Inspiration will flow through you like a fountain."

"A human life is formed by the combination of the physical from the earth and the spirit from the sky. The integration of the formed and unformed energies brings about the life of people. When the harmony of both in a person is maintained, then life is secured. If disharmony occurs internally in a person, then the life is troubled.

"In observing harmony, there is nothing to see and nothing to tell. By pacifying and guiding the emotions to embrace oneself in one's life being, longevity becomes possible. If the mind is expanded, one's internal life energy will be strong.

"The form of life persists when embracing the great one and ignoring the manifold differences of small and trivial matters and things. Do not be motivated by profit. Do not be afraid when trouble is seen. Be relaxed in Tao with spiritual confidence. Thus, one enjoys one's life, and the spiritual energy, like Heaven, lives within you."

"Life must be lived with joy. Vexation can cause disorder. Anger can cause a person to lose one's original, good direction. Harboring worry, sorrow, pleasure and anger causes one's mind to become cluttered and it then does not have room for Tao - the unity of life.

"Strong desires should be channelled. Restless impulses must be quietly guided.

"When a thing has not yet happened, do not use your mind to urge its arrival. Let blessings come to you by themselves.

"When a thing has already happened, do not use your mind to push it away.

"When a thing comes to you, your mind should attend to it with clarity. With no personal or internal struggle and with quietude of mind, you will act correctly. With impatience of mind, you will do poorly. Spiritual energy comes and goes as the gain or loss of your handling of a matter.

"In spiritual attainment, there is nothing further inside its smallness. There is also nothing further outside its largeness. The attainment of spiritual energy cannot be measured. It can be lost through the error of being impatient.

"If the mind abides in quiet, Tao is there. A person of Tao lives a life of self-generation. There is no projection of the future in his mind."

"By converging one's spiritual essence, one can know all.

"By concentration, one can know what will happen without the need of divination.

"By stopping one's searching, one will enjoy contentment without relying on external satisfaction.

"By constant thinking, the spirits will inspire you. This is possible by nurturing your own spiritual energy.

"By sitting upright, the circulation of blood will be fluent.

"By holding to a single purpose, not allowing the eyes and ears to be divided, things far away can be known as if near."

"When one's mind is governed, all other functions of the body are governed. When one's mind is at ease, all other functions of the body will be at ease. What governs the mind and what eases the mind? There is a higher mind within the mind. To be with the high mind is to be with spiritual essence."

"Do not allow externals to disturb the bodily function. Do not let the bodily function disturb the mind. This is internal harmony."

"When the lower mind reaches the highest essence of the mind, it lights up all darkness. When the searching mind knows to rest at the spiritual essence it has reached, it has attained enlightenment and maturity."

"After achieving harmony externally, the mind returns to its center. Thus, form and spiritual essence protect each other. Stay with oneness and never allow it to become dualistic. The person who can do this knows Tao."

"The gain or loss of Tao, the integral life being, is connected with the communication between the mind and its spirit. If the spirit is not connected, the integral life being is not complete. Communication between the life form and the life spirit takes place at the subtle conjunction made by the accord between Heaven and man.

"The completeness of life is the shared hope of the visible body and invisible mind and spirits. Great responsibility for meeting this goal rests on the control of the wandering mind.

"Therefore, let the mind experience the subtle truth and become a companion of Heaven. Instead of being occupied with worldly concepts and emotions, let free communication occur naturally and automatically, without even the slightest elusive movement of the mind. Mental activity disturbs the wholly expanded peace of each life's heavenly king. The intercourse of one's mind and one's spiritual essence is the true, deep benefit of spiritual self-achievement."

"Tao is the deepest union of all essences. Its root, trunk, leaves and flowers are not visible as with ordinary trees. It is the subtle potency of the deepest life of nature.

"People begin their lives in Tao, but they cannot keep to it as they proceed in life. Once the separation is widened, the union usually does not return. Occasionally, the spiritual union may come back but it does not stay, for people do not conform their lives to Tao. Instead, they conform their lives to their own internal and external creations.

"Be quiet, make no deviation, and the mind will meet the union of all subtle essences in one's life-being. The union has no form that can be seen, yet it can truly be achieved in our lives. It is truly with our lives. What sees no form, hears no sound, yet subtly assists the accomplishment of our life: This is Tao."

"Tao has no particular location.   It stays in a peaceful place. It stays with a peaceful mind. When one's mind is quiet and energy is reintegrated, normalcy is channeled and Tao is there. Tao is not far from people. It is what supports all lives. Tao does not separate. People cannot become wise without having attained Tao.

"Tao can be attained by spiritual development. The subtle integration is far reaching. Boundless, Tao is inexhaustible. The subtle integration cannot be attained by impulsive actions. It can only be attained by cultivating the nature of the mind and quieting ambition."

"Tao is unspeakable by the mouth, invisible to the eyes, inaudible to the ears. With the wholeness of life-essence, one attains the wholeness of the subtle life of nature."

"People will die by losing it.
People will live by attaining it.
People fail when they become emotional
    in the struggle for soul saving and
    personal security.
People succeed when they embrace the
    wholeness and naturalness of life within."

CHAPTER TWENTY

Being the Truth

The Purpose of Life
of the Student of Spiritual Development is:

To increase
the good life of all lives.

The Mission of Life
of the Students of Spiritual Development is:

To continue
the life of the universe.

The Meaning of Life

All students of spiritual development know
that a meaningful life is to:

Let your life be the essence of nature.
Let your heart be the conscience of mankind.
Let your soul be the light of the world.
Let your work continue the achievement
of all human ancestors.
Let your spirit stand
where all people can meet harmoniously.

Life is where spirits converge with good purpose.
Life is not where our spirit scatters
from base interests.
Immortality is not a carrot on the end of a stick.
Immortality is the foundation of our life evolution.

CHAPTER TWENTY-ONE

The Means must meet the Purpose

"The student of spiritual development watches to be sure the purpose and the means are right and the timing and circumstances are correct before he makes a move. Even if he is the right person in the right place, if the timing is wrong or the circumstance is not favorable, his endeavor will not succeed. Even if successful ends can be reached by evil means, he will not do it. In circumstances of cooperation, to insure the success of the endeavor, he needs to be sure that everyone involved is at a life stage compatible with whatever needs to be accomplished."

"A person with a mature or square personality who always keeps to the highest principles of ethics in his behavior and who strengthens his life being is admirable and worthy of praise. Square or mature behavior prevents the forming of weak spots.

"A person with a square personality should guard against being tricked by disguised people of inferior character.

"A person of straight character can be fooled by underdeveloped people who take advantage of his straightness and honesty. Thus, when straightness is applied, it should be with tactful manners rather than be an offensive move. One's good nature should never be an unguarded treasure.

"A student of spiritual development maintains an alert mind when facing a new or old situation and does not allow his square and straight nature to fall into a trap created by cunning or immature minds.

"A student of spiritual development is watchful in a situation where it is appropriate to practice kindness. He does not allow an evil hunter to prey on his good nature.

"A student of spiritual development is courageous and decisive in turning away from any situation in which his virtuous character would become a victim of someone else's evil plans.

"Although a student of spiritual development keeps himself alert on most occasions lest there be some harm done to him by something or someone, he does not allow himself a motivation that would harm other people, not even for one moment.

"When a person achieves high spirituality, he is not definable. He remains in a flexible position. He cannot be backed into a corner.

"When a person reaches maturity, his square and straight personality is not abrasive to others, because he is no longer sharp-cutting, pointed or stinging.

"Thus, the old master said: One who has attained the integral truth in his life cannot be categorized. He might be described, reluctantly, as follows:

"He who has attained the integral truth is cautious in conducting his life as though he were wading barefoot in a winter stream on slippery, mossy stones which might cause him to fall. His mind is always centered, like a kingdom which is alerted to the aggressive neighboring countries surrounding in all four directions. He is absolutely self-managed, so he is always proper, as though he were facing respected guests. At the same time that he is proper, he also flows very smoothly with the world and other people, like melting ice in the warm spring.

"He is simple and honest. Like a piece of untouched raw material, he is ready to accommodate himself to any situation. He is deep and inexhaustible like a wide valley or a deep ravine. In life experiences, he seems able to harmonize with all things, like the water of a long river that passes through different environments, picking up whatever the surroundings give to it. By remaining calm and still and letting the sediment settle, he does not suffer from any contamination. Thus, no outside impurity can remain with him to destroy or corrupt his spiritual essence.

"He is not shaken by disturbance or turmoil because he keeps nurturing his profound peace and unshakable independence; this puts him above the disturbance and turmoil of the world. The ease and composure of his deep spirit is unsurpassable and indestructible. It pacifies the disturbance and turmoil in his surroundings.

"His deepest spirit dwells in the depth of the valley. His detachment overcomes all obstacles. His deep spirit is always triumphant by dwelling in the center of non-competition, non-contention and non-compulsion. It is the very core of nature.

"One who conforms his life to Tao, the integral truth, does not overextend himself. Because he does not overextend in anything, he is always able to renew himself. Thus, his life remains forever fresh and he is not exhausted by the internal and external situations in his life."

"One student of spiritual development asked his teacher: 'Is spiritual development a process for all general people to use at the stage of naivete in order to develop into the stage of maturity, at the stage of innocence to develop into the stage of sophistication, and at the stage of ignorance to develop into the stage of wisdom?'

"The teacher answered, 'The development you ask about concerns the processes of the intellectual mind and psychological matters. Spiritual development is different. Naivete and innocence are considered the highest treasure of human spiritual nature. When people experience the world, their naivete and innocence could be lost totally. In spiritual development, the goal is that whatever one experiences in life, good or bad, happy or painful, etc., one does not let his naive and innocent nature become destroyed or damaged by that experience. Surely, experiences may cause temporary pain or unhappiness, but the person of spiritual development returns to a state of openness and awareness, and remains spiritually unaffected by the experience. Thus he is an untwisted and unpressed person of wholeness. The experiences are acknowledged and understood for what they are.

"'If one's unaffected nature or naivete and innocence is totally destroyed, one's spiritual essence dies. There would hardly be the possibility of spiritual rejuvenation. However, ignorance is the defect of one's spiritual nature, while wisdom is the cure. The attainment of wisdom, however, is still at a less profound level than the naive, innocent and always renewable core of the spiritual center. This is an important understanding for spiritual development.

"'This means that when you develop your mind with worldly knowledge, wisdom, sophistication, maturity, etc., at the same time, you keep your pristine nature unharmed and intact. That is the correct process of spiritual growth.

"'When a teaching is given to intellectually developed people during this time of intellectual dominance, one can engage in intellectual discussion. However, this keeps one on the superficial, "skin-deep" level which is still a long way from the spiritual core of life.'

"'Can the definite goal of spiritual development be known by us?' the student requested to know.

"'Let me repeat the goal of spiritual development of the original Taoists, people of Integral Truth:

"'1)   Are your body and spirit united perfectly without being in conflict or separating from each other, so that no divergence is caused by different life stages or by different spiritual or physical interests?

"'2)   Can you concentrate on nurturing your essence to achieve harmony with your environment and, at the same time, cause no conflict in other people's lives, by being as selfless or pure as a baby?

"'3)   Can you eliminate the absent, scattered mind and keep a deep and quiet observation over your own life and your surroundings without the slightest obstruction of preconception or subjectivity?

"'4)   Do you love people and support the orderliness of the world without extending your personal ambition, expansion, or exaltation over others and the world?

"'5)   When you discover you are in a confrontation with a life opportunity of another, can you remain yourself and be understanding and flexible? If it is necessary, can you practice the principle of feminine yielding and give up the masculine tendency to assert one's personal advantage, and let the other person be the winner with your permission?   (This means you give up being like a fiery, fighting bull.)

"'6) Can you achieve crystal clarity, making no interference with the natural development of your internal growth and the growth of your surroundings?

"'7)   Can you support the positive growth of all in your surroundings without requiring any of them to be yours or take credit for it?

"'8)   When you are able to bring about an achievement which benefits all, or you promote a healthy and orderly world, can you refrain from extending your personal interest in becoming the leader or the boss of that group?

"'These goals cover your internal and external spiritual development.   They are not fanciful achievements, yet they can be realized only as one attains spiritual development.'"

"Another student asked: 'It seems that life is so hard.   There is no fun or pleasure included in this, or any other, spiritual instruction you have given.'

"The teacher smiled and answered: 'Do you know what fun is?   When one abides in naivete and innocence, joy grows from within.   When the mind becomes too complicated and sophisticated, simple fun can no longer be satisfying, then harmful fun is invented.   To maintain naivete and innocence is to truly enjoy life.

"'Personally, I do not look for fun. When the fun comes, I enjoy it. If one looks for fun or creates fun, it is not fun. It loses its quality from the extra labor. When fun comes by itself, alongside the main direction in your life, you enjoy it. Then you can include it as a part of your life. Besides that, life itself and work are fun, too. A healer helps sick people become well. A mechanic fixes up whatever comes to his hand, etc. Is that not fun? In everyday life, if you walk a couple of miles, grow flowers or fruit in your back yard, etc., is that not fun, too? Most healthy, creative activities are fun.

"'It is as the old master taught: life is complete and joyful. Beyond accomplishing the basic needs of your life, to look for achievement or excitement is an unnecessary addition to life. Thus, he teaches no extra doing in achieving your life.'"

"A person who can thoroughly understand and take in the teachings of this ageless tradition, which was motivated solely by the pursuit of immortal life, and adhere to its guidelines, will find that his life will be fulfilled naturally. After he has had enough worldly experience to help him attain spiritual awareness of life, the suitable study for this special individual whose life expression is Tao and Teh, would be Lao Tzu's *Tao Teh Ching* and related material, with its important heritage of development.

"*Ching* means guidance. *Teh* means the inner virtue of the individual. Teh is the equivalence of internal worth and internal strength that keeps one from being bent or manipulated by any external evil influence. It means that one's life or behavior does not originate from internal or external pressures, but rather from natural harmony or achieved internal and external harmony. This is attainment. Thus, it is Teh. Teh, practically, means spiritual gain.

"Behavior from inside that outwardly reaches harmony with the subtle law of nature is Tao. After you have attained this harmony, you can open up totally to appreciate the spiritual being and direction described in the *Complete Works of Lao Tzu* which is the highest spiritual direction and destination of all people who have attained the highest spiritual awareness."

Afterword

It is easy for people, before attaining spiritual development, to become troubled. If your friend is beautiful, but her life is not supported by a healthy personality, her beauty would become a poison.

If your friend is in a powerful position, but he does not have a healthy personality, his power could be poison to himself and other people.

If your friend is very rich, but he does not have a healthy personality, his riches could become a poison for him and his children too.

If your friend is one of the leaders of an extreme ideology, though he speaks convincingly, if his character is not supported by a basic healthy personality, the capability he possesses would be a poison to himself and poison to people.

It does not matter how people are related to you; even if they are as close as father and son, mother and daughter or brother and sister, if the other person does not have a well-balanced, healthy personality, the relationship must be a bitter one.

Therefore, if we have a troubled world, it must be because there are many troubled individuals. Why are there so many? It is because they have not been directed or educated or inspired to attain a healthy personality. Once they realize the healthy growth of their original personality, they become precious, not only good for themselves, but very precious for the world. It is a wish that this book will serve as a mirror to you so you can see who you are and where you are now.

If you have a lot of money, you can buy the many things that you may want. There are also many kinds of services available to you. Let us take, for example, medical services. Whatever trouble you may have, there is always a medical professional to serve your need. If you have an unattractive nose, a plastic surgeon can help to make you look better. If your teeth are crooked, the orthodontist will make your teeth look nice, look better. If you are psychologically weak or troubled, there are also professional psychologists to help you. There is also help for your parents, your house, your car, your garden. There is always someone who is a specialist to help you with your troubles. We have become too focused upon outward help, looking for something to assist us with our many problems, but there is no immediate service to cure an undeveloped personality.

The world is composed of people. The world situation reflects the quality of people on the planet. It is by building your own healthy personality that you serve the world by helping the world attain its health.

A person whose personality is strong and healthy, even if he is physically sick, is still more valuable than a person whose personality is sick. A person whose personality is healthy, even if he is poor, is still more helpful and beneficial than a rich person whose personality is unhealthy and unbalanced. A person whose personality is healthy, even if he is in a low position, is still more useful than a person with an unhealthy personality in an important, high position. If one's personality is not healthy and he is standing on a platform before the public, he will poison the people with bad ideas. If a person does not have a healthy personality, he cannot be a good teacher or salesperson, or anything else. Whatever position he is in, he will be the troublemaker or harm-giver.

Without a healthy personality, a policeman might turn out to be a criminal; he would not bring any good to society but only cause trouble. Therefore, the attainment of a healthy personality is important for everyone. When you do yourself good, you do the world good. When you do not do yourself good, there is nothing you can do for the world that is good. There are profound, complicated and lofty ideologies in spiritual teaching, but if they do not help to build healthy personalities among all people and instead teach prejudice, they are not helpful to people and the world.

When people do not work to attain healthy personalties, their stagnant emotion would rot their personality. They are rotten inside and outside, too, from external influences. How can you promote that they to go to heaven? What do you promote, their waiting for a messiah to come and save their souls? Is this not a deception? Basically, they have become rotten. When the world has become rotten, who will bring about a paradise on earth and who shall enjoy it?

Unless people have their own spiritual awareness and attain healthy personalities, they cannot enjoy a healthy world. And if they do not enjoy the world, what can they enjoy?

For almost two thousand years, religions have promoted their untruthful ideology among people. Such political promotion tends to foster extreme ideologies. Do you see how the health of the world becomes where people are educated to see only the temporary benefit or profit they can grab? However, they cannot see the poison that seeps deeply into their bones from their attitude. When such a cultural trend continues, the world itself finally becomes rotten and decayed.

People who have an unhealthy character are dangerous to approach. They are dangerous to be close to. Suppose your boyfriend or girlfriend has AIDS? Even if he or she is a good person, what is lacking is some knowledge about sexual hygiene. But having a low character is worse than having AIDS. Would you like to contact a person who has a worse condition than AIDS? AIDS is curable at a certain stage and someday it will be totally curable by modern or ancient natural medicinal systems. But a low character or ignoble personality cannot be cured unless the person himself decides that it is not beneficial for him to continue with this pattern. He can only be cured when he decides to attain his own growth and do better in his life.

You know the value of a good personality. It is worthy for all of us to confirm our commitment to a healthy way of life. You do not need to depend on an external evaluation to decide your worth. People should evaluate themselves each moment because by doing so, they are able to make progress in their lives.

We do not like to live in suppressed circumstances or be shaped by external forces, but we need to exert subjective effort to turn around our spiritual evolution from downfall to upward and onward again.

It has been my personal dedication since I was very little to prepare this large amount of material that has been put together for you to learn Tao: physical fitness, psychological fitness and spiritual fitness all together in one whole. This was my own learning; it is not my own invention. These important teachings came through generations of people who devoted their lifetimes and energies to achieving themselves.

I dedicate this book to the health of people and the health of the world. Healthy people occasionally have an illness in some small area of their lives; it is easy to fix when they have the self-awareness and the spiritual alertness to facilitate an immediate cure. I also offer these books to people, who having experienced the unhealthy world, are seeking to re-enforce their lives to resist the bad influences. Of course this book is dedicated to them more than to anyone who merely looks for spiritual fantasy instead of realistic spiritual improvement. People looking for realistic improvement are the gold of the world. They are the pearls of human society. They are ones who can use the help the most and who will help the world.

After my work of distillation of much material, I would like to recommend the following guidelines to you for your study.

1) It is helpful to study the *Book of Changes and the Unchanging Truth.* The *Book of Changes and the Unchanging Truth* has been proven to be useful and effective in educating an individual's total life.

2) Once you have completed the wide reading of all my books, if you like, use the *Workbook for Spiritual Development of All People.* It is best to use it every day to channel the scattering energy of your spirit and mind. Doing this will greatly benefit you.

3) If you are serious, you should consider adopting some of the life advice from the two volumes of *8,000 Years of Wisdom,* especially in the areas of diet and sex.

4) It is suggested that you learn Chi Gong, Tai Chi or Dou In, Eight Treasures and other martial arts. Physical movement can improve your health and, thus support your spiritual achievement.

5) It is helpful to have a basic understanding of the principles of nutrition. This knowledge has been compiled in the *Tao of Nutrition*.

6) Study internal alchemy. It is presented in the *Story of Two Kingdoms*.

7) Once in a while, if you are troubled physically or if you need to do a seasonal purification of the toxins you have gathered in daily life, it is suggested that natural herbs or acupuncture might be used to help you. Seek out good books for a better understanding and a professional acupuncturist for assistance.

8) It is suggested that you know something about your personal life pattern and cycles. An achieved Taoist astrologer can tell you with great accuracy how your life patterns and energy cycles manifest. A good interpretation of such a chart depends on the skill and achievement of the astrologer, whatever his or her school. If achieved, they can accurately tell you what to avoid and where to go forward, and how to channel your lifestyle and personal energy. They can tell you which energies are favorable for you to develop, in which direction to manage your higher development and which style of life is helpful for you.

9) Conform yourself to the law of balanced behavior in the *Stepping Stones for Spiritual Success*, if

you wish someday to live a worry-less life or in a worry-less world.

10) It is helpful to begin the practice of meditation in whatever way you can. Skill and inspiration in meditation will come to you. Success takes commitment, so begin with a short time period, if you must, and let the constancy of practice become your good habit.

11) Pay attention to the teaching that comes to you in your everyday life. You will find inspiring teachings, informal rather than formal, everywhere if you are open to them, once you nurture the sensitivity of your spiritual energy. They come disguised as events, situations, gifts, people, environments, jobs, objects, difficulties and thoughts, etc. Your life is your teacher and my books with their recommended practices will help you learn.

For example, by showing you that yin and yang are two different manifestations of one great energy, both positive and seemingly negative happenings can be recognized to great advantage in your learning. So, be open to what comes to you, and ask yourself, "What is the lesson that I can learn from this? What is my relationship to this? What can this show me about the truth?" More importantly, the right inspiration will come to you according to the stage of life you are in and your level of spiritual development.

12) If you have the interest and if your life situation allows you the time, it is always beneficial for you to read many good books. This helps you to make progress and see how much progress you have made. Scatteredness bears no fruit. Unless you have already been reading carefully through many

good books and learning from other teachings, you will not know the great value in what you have now reached. There are some things in my books that your mind may not catch at first. Read them over after you attain more life experience. Then, the same old books can refresh and inspire you.

13) If you understand that traveling to other places can help you gather knowledge and personal experience on one level, you can also see that spiritual learning must be done in a quieter place where you can come into yourself deeply.

14) Once you have read and wandered widely, you will know which things you would like to stay with and keep as your personal direction for study.

Before, you were at the fence. You will soon be at the gate. Maybe you will want to enter the hall. Perhaps you would like to go to the outer room and then to sit in the inner room and enjoy the use of the invaluable treasures.

BOOKS IN ENGLISH BY MASTER NI

Stepping Stones for Spiritual Success - New Publication - In Asia, the custom of foot binding was followed for close to a thousand years. In the West, people did not practice foot binding, but they bound their thoughts, for a much longer period, some 1,500 to 1,700 years. Their mind and thinking became unnatural. Being unnatural expresses a state of confusion where people do not know what is right. Once they become natural again, they become clear and progress is great. Master Ni invites his readers to unbind their minds; in this volume, he has taken the best of the traditional teachings and put them in to contemporary language to make them more relevant to our time, culture and lives. Stock No. BSTE.

The Complete Works of Lao Tzu
Lao Tzu's Tao Teh Ching is one of the most widely translated and cherished works of literature in the world. It presents the core of Taoist philosophy. Lao Tzu's timeless wisdom provides a bridge to the subtle spiritual truth as well as practical guidelines for harmonious and peaceful living. Master Ni has included what is believed to be the only English translation of the Hua Hu Ching, a later work of Lao Tzu which has been lost to the general public for a thousand years. 212 pages, 1986. Stock No. BCOM. Softcover, $9.50

Order The Complete Works of Lao Tzu and the companion Tao Teh Ching Cassette Tapes for only $20.00. Stock No. ABLAO.

The Book of Changes and the Unchanging Truth
The first edition of this book was widely appreciated by its readers, who drew great spiritual benefit from it. They found the principles of the I Ching to be clearly explained and useful to their lives, especially the helpful commentaries. The legendary classic I Ching is recognized as mankind's first written book of wisdom. Leaders and sages throughout history have consulted it as a trusted advisor which reveals the appropriate action to be taken in any of life's circumstances. This volume also includes over 200 pages of background material on Taoist principles of natural energy cycles, instruction and commentaries. New, revised second edition, 669 pages, 1990. Stock No. BBOO. Hardcover, $35.00

The Story of Two Kingdoms
This volume is the metaphoric tale of the conflict between the Kingdoms of Light and Darkness. Through this unique story, Master Ni transmits the esoteric teachings of Taoism which have been carefully guarded secrets for over 5,000 years. This book is for those who are serious in their search and have devoted their lives to achieving high spiritual goals. 122 pages, 1989. Stock No. BSTO. Hardcover, $14.00

The Way of Integral Life

This book can help build a bridge for those wishing to connect spiritual and intellectual development. It is most helpful for modern educated people. It includes practical and applicable suggestions for daily life, philosophical thought, esoteric insight and guidelines for those aspiring to give help and service to the world. This book helps you learn the wisdom of the ancient sages' achievement to assist the growth of your own wisdom and integrate it as your own new light and principles for balanced, reasonable living in worldly life. 320 pages, 1989. Softcover, $14.00, Stock No. BWAYS. Hardcover, $20.00, Stock No. BWAYH

Enlightenment: Mother of Spiritual Independence

The inspiring story and teachings of Master Hui Neng, the father of Zen Buddhism and Sixth Patriarch of the Buddhist tradition, highlight this volume. Hui Neng was a person of ordinary birth, intellectually unsophisticated, who achieved himself to become a spiritual leader. Master Ni includes enlivening commentaries and explanations of the principles outlined by this spiritual revolutionary. Having received the same training as all Zen Masters as one aspect of his training and achievement, Master Ni offers this teaching so that his readers may be guided in their process of spiritual development. 264 pages, 1989 Softcover, $12.50, Stock No. BENLS. Hardcover, $18.00, Stock No. BENLH

Attaining Unlimited Life

The thought-provoking teachings of Chuang Tzu are presented in this volume. He was perhaps the greatest philosopher and master of Taoism and he laid the foundation for the Taoist school of thought. Without his work, people of later generations would hardly recognize the value of Lao Tzu's teaching in practical, everyday life. He touches the organic nature of human life more deeply and directly than that of other great teachers. This volume also includes questions by students and answers by Master Ni. 467 pages, 1989. Softcover, $18.00, Stock No. BATTS; Hardcover, $25.00, Stock No. BATTH

The Gentle Path of Spiritual Progress

This book offers a glimpse into the dialogues of a Taoist master with the public. In a relaxed, open manner, Master Ni, Hua-Ching explains the fundamental practices that are the keys to experiencing enlightenment in everyday life. Many of the traditional secrets of Taoist training are revealed. People also ask a surprising range of questions, and Master Ni's answers touch on contemporary psychology, finances, sexual advice, how to use the I Ching as well as the telling of some fascinating Taoist legends. Softcover, $12.50, Stock No. BGEN

Spiritual Messages from a Buffalo Rider, A Man of Tao
This is another important collection of Master Ni's service in his worldly trip, originally published as one half of The Gentle Path. He had the opportunity to meet people and answer their questions to help them gain the spiritual awareness that we live at the command of our animal nature. Our buffalo nature rides on us, whereas an achieved person rides the buffalo. In this book, Master Ni gives much helpful knowledge to those who are interested in improving their lives and deepening their cultivation so they too can develop beyond their mundane beings. Softcover, $12.50, Stock No. BSPI

8,000 Years of Wisdom, Volume I and II
This two volume set contains a wealth of practical, down-to-earth advice given by Master Ni to his students over a five year period, 1979 to 1983. Drawing on his training in Traditional Chinese Medicine, Herbology, Acupuncture and other Taoist arts, Master Ni gives candid answers to students' questions on many topics ranging from dietary guidance to sex and pregnancy, meditation techniques and natural cures for common illnesses. Volume I includes dietary guidance; 236 pages; Stock No. BEIG1 Volume II includes sex and pregnancy guidance; 241 pages; Stock No. BEIG2. 1983, Softcover, Each Volume $12.50

The Uncharted Voyage Towards the Subtle Light
Spiritual life in the world today has become a confusing mixture of dying traditions and radical novelties. People who earnestly and sincerely seek something more than just a way to fit into the complexities of a modern structure that does not support true self-development often find themselves spiritually struggling. This book provides a profound understanding and insight into the underlying heart of all paths of spiritual growth, the subtle origin and the eternal truth of one universal life. 424 pages, 1985. Stock No. BUNC. Softcover, $14.50

The Heavenly Way
A translation of the classic Tai Shan Kan Yin Pien (Straighten Your Way) and Yin Chia Wen (The Silent Way of Blessing). The treaties in this booklet are the main guidance for a mature and healthy life. The purpose of this booklet is to promote the recognition of truth, because only truth can teach the perpetual Heavenly Way by which one reconnects oneself with the divine nature. 41 pages, 1981; Stock No. BHEA. Softcover, $2.50

Footsteps of the Mystical Child
This book poses and answers such questions as: What is a soul? What is wisdom? What is spiritual evolution? The answers to these and many other questions enable readers to open themselves to new realms of understanding and personal growth. There are also many true examples about people's internal and external struggles on the path of self-development and spiritual evolution. 166 pages, 1986; Stock No. BFOO. Softcover, $9.50

Workbook for Spiritual Development
This book offers a practical, down-to-earth, hands-on approach for those who are devoted to the path of spiritual achievement. The reader will find diagrams showing fundamental hand positions to increase and channel one's spiritual energy, postures for sitting, standing and sleeping cultivation as well as postures for many Taoist invocations. The material in this workbook is drawn from the traditional teachings of Taoism and summarizes thousands of years of little known practices for spiritual development. An entire section is devoted to ancient invocations, another on natural celibacy and another on postures. In addition, Master Ni explains the basic attitudes and understandings that are the foundation for Taoist practices. 224 pages, 1984. Stock No. BWOR. Softcover, $12.50

Poster of Master Lu
Color poster of Master Lu, Tung Ping (shown on cover of workbook), for use with the workbook or in one's shrine. 16" x 22"; Stock No. POS. $10.00

The Taoist Inner View of the Universe
This presentation of Taoist metaphysics provides guidance for one's own personal life transformation. Master Ni has given all the opportunity to know the vast achievement of the ancient unspoiled mind and its transpiercing vision. This book offers a glimpse of the inner world and immortal realm known to achieved Taoists and makes it understandable for students aspiring to a more complete life. 218 pages, 1979. Stock No. BTAOI. Softcover, $12.50

Tao, the Subtle Universal Law
Most people are unaware that their thoughts and behavior evoke responses from the invisible net of universal energy. The real meaning of Taoist self-discipline is to harmonize with universal law. To lead a good stable life is to be aware of the actual conjoining of the universal subtle law with every moment of our lives. This book presents the wisdom and practical methods that the ancient Chinese have successfully used for centuries to accomplish this. 165 pages, 1979. Stock No. TAOS. Softcover, $7.50

MATERIALS ON TAOIST HEALTH, ARTS AND SCIENCES

BOOKS

The Tao of Nutrition by Maoshing Ni, Ph.D., with Cathy McNease, B.S., M.H. - Working from ancient Chinese medical classics and contemporary research, Dr. Maoshing Ni and Cathy McNease have compiled an indispensable guide to natural healing. This exceptional book shows the reader how to take control of one's health through one's eating habits. This volume contains 3 major sections: the first section deals with theories of Chinese nutrition and philosophy; the second describes over 100 common foods in detail, listing their energetic properties, therapeutic actions and individual remedies. The third section lists nutritional remedies for many common ailments. This book presents both a healing system and a disease prevention system which is flexible in adapting to every individual's needs. 214 pages, 1987. Stock No. BTAON. Softcover, $14.50

Chinese Vegetarian Delights by Lily Chuang
An extraordinary collection of recipes based on principles of traditional Chinese nutrition. Many recipes are therapeutically prepared with herbs. Diet has long been recognized as a key factor in health and longevity. For those who require restricted diets and those who choose an optimal diet, this cookbook is a rare treasure. Meat, sugar, diary products and fried foods are excluded. Produce, grains, tofu, eggs and seaweeds are imaginatively prepared. 104 pages, 1987. Stock No. BCHIV. Softcover, $7.50

Chinese Herbology Made Easy - by Maoshing Ni, Ph.D.
This text provides an overview of Oriental medical theory, in-depth descriptions of each herb category, with over 300 black and white photographs, extensive tables of individual herbs for easy reference, and an index of pharmaceutical and Pin-Yin names. The distillation of overwhelming material into essential elements enables one to focus efficiently and develop a clear understanding of Chinese herbology. This book is especially helpful for those studying for their California Acupuncture License. 202 pages, 1986. Stock No. BCHIH. Softcover, 14.50

Crane Style Chi Gong Book - By Daoshing Ni, Ph.D.
Chi Gong is a set of meditative exercises that was developed several thousand years ago by Taoists in China. It is now practiced for healing purposes, combining breathing techniques, body movements and mental imagery to guide the smooth flow of energy throughout the body. This book gives a more detailed account and study of Chi Gong than the videotape alone. It may be used with or without the videotape. Includes complete instructions and information on using Chi Gong exercise as a medical therapy. 55 pages, 1984. Stock No. BCRA. Spiral bound $10.00

VIDEO TAPES

Crane Style Chi Gong *(VHS) by Dr. Daoshing Ni, Ph.D.*
Chi Gong is a set of meditative exercises developed several thousand years ago by ancient Taoists in China. It is now practiced for healing stubborn chronic diseases, strengthening the body to prevent disease and as a tool for further spiritual enlightenment. It combines breathing techniques, simple body movements, and mental imagery to guide the smooth flow of energy throughout the body. Chi gong is easy to learn for all ages. Correct and persistent practice will increase one's energy, relieve stress or tension, improve concentration and clarity, release emotional stress and restore general well-being. 2 hours Stock No. VCRA. $65.00

Eight Treasures *(VHS) - By Maoshing Ni, Ph.D.*
These exercises help open blocks in a person's energy flow and strengthen one's vitality. It is a complete exercise combining physical stretching and toning and energy conducting movements coordinated with breathing. The Eight Treasures are an exercise unique to the Ni family. Patterned from nature, the 32 movements of the Eight Treasures are an excellent foundation for Tai Chi Chuan or martial arts. 1 hour and 45 minutes. Stock No. VEIG. $49.00

Tai Chi Chuan - I & II *(VHS) By Maoshing Ni, Ph.D.*
This exercise integrates the flow of physical movement with that of integral energy in the Taoist style of "Harmony," similar to the long form of Yang-style Tai Chi Chuan. Tai Chi has been practiced for thousands of years to help both physical longevity and spiritual cultivation. 1 hour each. Each Video Tape $49.00. Order both for $90.00. Stock Nos: Part I, VTAI1; Part II, VTAI2; Set of two, VTAISET.

AUDIO CASSETTES

Invocations: Health and Longevity and Healing a Broken Heart *By Maoshing Ni, Ph.D. This audio cassette guides the listener through a series of ancient invocations to channel and conduct one's own healing energy and vital force. "Thinking is louder than thunder." The mystical power by which all miracles are brought about is your sincere practice of this principle. 30 minutes. Stock No. AINV. $5.95*

Chi Gong for Stress Release *By Maoshing Ni, Ph.D.*
This audio cassette guides you through simple, ancient breathing exercises that enable you to release day-to-day stress and tension that are such a common cause of illness today. 30 minutes. Stock No. ACHIS. $8.95

Chi Gong for Pain Management By Maoshing Ni, Ph.D.
Using easy visualization and deep-breathing techniques that have been developed over thousands of years, this audio cassette offers methods for overcoming pain by invigorating your energy flow and unblocking obstructions that cause pain. 30 minutes. Stock No. ACHIP. $8.95

Tao Teh Ching Cassette Tapes
This classic work of Lao Tzu has been recorded in this two-cassette set that is a companion to the book translated by Master Ni. Professionally recorded and read by Robert Rudelson. 120 minutes. Stock No. ATAO. $12.00

Order Master Ni's book, *The Complete Works of Lao Tzu*, and Tao Teh Ching Cassette Tapes for only $20.00. Stock No. ABLAO.

How To Order

Complete this form and mail it to: **Union of Tao and Man,**
117 Stonehaven Way, Los Angeles, CA 90049 (213)-472-9970

Name:

Address:

City: State: Zip:

Phone - Daytime: Evening:

(We may telephone you if we have questions about your order.)

Qty.	Stock No.	Title/Description	Price Each	Total Price

Total amount for items ordered_____

Sales tax (CA residents, 6-1/2%)_____

Shipping Charge (See below)_____

Total Amount Enclosed_____

Please allow 6 - 8 weeks for delivery.
Thank you for your order.

U. S. Funds Only, Please
Please write your check or money order
to Union of Tao and Man

Shipping Charge - All Orders Sent Via U.S. Postal Service, unless specified.
Domestic Surface Mail: First item $2.00, each additional, add $.50.
Canada Surface Mail: First item $2.50, each additional, add $1.00.
Other Foreign Surface Mail: First item $3.00, each additional, add $2.00.
Foreign Air Mail: First item $18.00, each additional, add $7.00.

Spiritual Study Through the College of Tao

The College of Tao and the Union of Tao and Man were established formally in California in the 1970's. This tradition is a very old spiritual culture of mankind, holding long experience of human spiritual growth. Its central goal is to offer healthy spiritual education to all people of our society. This time tested tradition values the spiritual development of each individual self and passes down its guidance and experience.

Master Ni carries his tradition from its country of origin to the west. He chooses to avoid making the mistake of old-style religions that have rigid establishments which resulted in fossilizing the delicacy of spiritual reality. Rather, he prefers to guide the teachings of his tradition as a school of no boundary rather than a religion with rigidity. Thus, the branches or centers of this Taoist school offer different programs of similar purpose. Each center extends its independent service, but all are unified in adopting Master Ni's work as the foundation of teaching to fulfill the mission of providing spiritual education to all people.

The centers offer their classes, teaching, guidance and practices on building the groundwork for cultivating a spiritually centered and well-balanced life. As a person obtains the correct knowledge with which to properly guide himself or herself, he or she can then become more skillful in handling the experiences of daily life. The assimilation of good guidance in one's practical life brings about different stages of spiritual development.

Any interested individual is welcome to join and learn to grow for oneself. You might like to join the center near where you live, or you yourself may be interested in organizing a center or study group based on the model of existing centers. In that way, we all work together for the spiritual benefit of all people. We do not require any religious type of commitment.

The learning is life. The development is yours. The connection of study may be helpful, useful and serviceable, directly to you.

- -

Mail to: Union of Tao and Man, 117 Stonehaven Way, Los Angeles, CA 90049

_____ I wish to be put on the mailing list of the Union of Tao and Man to be notified of classes, educational activities and new publications.

Name:_____

Address:_____

City:_____State:_____Zip:_____

INDEX